WAR FLYING IN MACEDONIA

v. Eschwege
Leutnant

WAR FLYING IN MACEDONIA

By
HAUPT HEYDEMARCK
Author of *Double-Decker C666* and *Flying Section 17*

Translated by
CLAUD W. SYKES

The Naval & Military Press Ltd

Published by

The Naval & Military Press Ltd
Unit 5 Riverside, Brambleside
Bellbrook Industrial Estate
Uckfield, East Sussex
TN22 1QQ England

Tel: +44 (0)1825 749494

www.naval–military–press.com
www.nmarchive.com

FOREWORD

CAPTAIN HEYDEMARCK'S request for a foreword to WAR FLYING IN MACEDONIA reached me via his translator and his publisher. It was accompanied by an advance copy of his book, which I have read with considerable interest and great pleasure. I have found his pages full of wholesome love of his work and a kindly feeling for those unfortunate airmen of all camps who faced the intense heat and cold, the mosquitos, the barrenness and hideousness of Macedonia and who fell or survived as the fortune of war dictated. My pilot (Sidney Beare) and myself were both fortunate and unfortunate, for we met in the air Lt. von Eschwege, the star scout pilot of Capt. Heydemarck's staffel. He was flying I believe a Halberstadt machine capable of doing 120 m.p.h. on the level and had the use of two guns synchronized with his propeller and he was a first class shot! Our Nieuport (new though it was) could achieve but 80 m.p.h. The odds were, of course, heavily against us and when Eschwege's bullets got through our gravity tank (not to mention our bodies) we had to land ; what a very skilful landing Captain Beare made in spite of his injuries ! We were, of course, in enemy territory. After a long delay we were taken to hospital at Boiran, thence later to Drama. Dr. Slavtcheff was the surgeon who attended to our wounds and he found it necessary to amputate my right foot. We shall always remember his kindness and sympathy to us in our sorry plight. After being discharged from hospital we were sent to Philipopolis, there to linger until the end of hostilities.

It is a far cry from a medical practice in a country

7

town in Staffordshire to Captain Heydemarck's office in Berlin, where he is now in business as a publisher and a very much farther cry to the Macedonia where we fought on opposite sides, but this book which is well translated and easy to read gives an accurate account of events that took place when I was an observer in No. 17 Squadron R.F.C. and revives memories which had been growing fainter and fainter. I can heartily recommend this book to any youngster who is air-minded. I hope that he or she will gather from it some sound and profitable advice as to the care of machines. The importance of spending time and care on aircraft by a very efficient personnel is stressed frequently and Lt. von Eschwege proved his all-round ability by personal attention to his machines on the ground, thus enabling him to secure a great measure of success in the air. There can be nothing better for an Air Force than pilots who understand and nurse their craft. Success is bound to follow. Apart from the love he lavished on his " buses," Sidney Beare and I will always remember Eschwege's solicitude for us and our wounds. He brought to us in hospital gifts of chocolate, books and cigarettes. Alas ! that he is dead. May his soul rest in peace after his many flights.

In conclusion I must thank the author and translator for the honour and kindness they have accorded me in asking my help for these prefatory remarks. I can only hope that in some small measure they will enhance the value of this very interesting volume, which gives such a vivid account of War Flying in a remote and undesirable corner of the world.

E. P. Hyde.

Lt. R.F.C.

17th Squadron.

CONTENTS

LIST OF ILLUSTRATIONS

CHAPTER I

ALL BEGINNINGS ARE DIFFICULT

UP to the end of 1916 I flew reconnaisances for Section 17 in the Champagne.[1] But after my friend, Take Engmann, had fallen in action, I went off

[1] See *Double Decker C.666* and *Flying Section* 17, published by John Hamilton, Ltd.

to southern Serbia, where my old C.O. had taken over
Flying Section 30, which was attached to the 1st
Bulgarian Army. I was able to report to Captain
Mohr at Hudova on the first day of the Christmas
holidays.

" Nice job for you, my dear fellow," he greeted
me. " We're the first section down here to get a
serial camera. You got used to this filming business
in the West, so you can get us going here."

.   .   .   .   .

The serial camera's machine—an Albatros with a 200
h.p. engine—stands ready to take off. I test my
machine gun as we roll up to the starting point—
O.K. ! When the mechanics withdraw, I bend over to
Sergeant Roth :

" Aren't you going to try your gun ? "

He shakes his head. " We don't do it until we are
in the air. We can blaze away anywhere in the
mountains—not a soul there."

Good enough for me. So I give him a nod, and we
whizz off. I settle down comfortably into my seat
and study the map. As Roth has been flying here for
a long time and knows the front thoroughly, it will
be an easy job to whack him on to the right course.

" Tacktacktacktack . . . "—ah, now he's getting his
trial shots in. The rattle seems to please him, for he
refuses to stop it. I bend over to him in surprise, but
he still ejects burst after burst.

Then the business gets a bit too thick for me. Those
are just the bullets we might want in a fight ! I give
him an irritated whack on his helmet and display my
annoyance in his mirror. But he shrugs his shoulders
and goes on shooting.

Has the fellow gone mad ? I lay a rough hand on his
right shoulder and threaten him with my fist because

the roar of the engine and the rattle of the machine gun make verbal communications impossible. But he shrugs his shoulders again and turns round so that I can see the helpless look in his eyes through the glass of his goggles. At the same moment he raises his right hand and points to the stick.

I perceive with horror that he is not pressing the trigger button. The mechanism of the trigger, which is regulated by the motion of the propeller, has got itself jammed—and now the bullets are chasing one another out of the barrel, and we have no means of stopping them. That is not the worst, however; if there was nothing else, we could land and look fools. But—and it makes my heart go hot and cold in turns—the action of the gun is no longer synchronized. Many bullets are passing through the wooden propeller blades instead of to one side of them!

Any second may bring the catastrophe. The propeller blades are still holding together, but sooner or later they must burst asunder, and if a large piece of wood hits a strut or a wing, the terrific speed at which it is travelling will produce the same effect as a hit by a shell-splinter and smash up the machine. Even if we are spared this calamity, the tragic fate of Immelmann still threatens us. In his case only one propeller blade broke away, but the uneven strain wrenched his engine from its bed—the machine broke up—and the cockpit carried Immelmann down to his death.

Then—an idea of salvation! I place my mouth against Roth's ear and scream through the hellish din: "Engine off!"

He shrugs his shoulders: "Can't hear you!"

Light dawns on him when I explain my meaning by gestures. His hand moves quickly to the switch.

The propeller's revolutions grow slower, as only the air-pressure moves it—but the machine-gun goes on shooting. Again and again Roth bangs at the mechanism in his efforts to cease fire—but in vain!

There is still a way out; if we cut the ignition, the propeller generally goes dead, especially if the glide is kept quite flat. I bend over again swiftly: "Ignition off!"

Roth turns the key to "Off." But—as we might expect—it fails to work this time. The air pressure keeps the propeller revolving, while the machine-gun continues to rattle away.

No other way out; we must submit to the Destiny which will decide the question of life or death for us in a few seconds. My heart is quite calm now. We can do nothing more to help ourselves—we must just wait, wait. The seconds drag out endlessly. My will revolts against this inactivity, but it is soon under control again. Wait, wait!

Perhaps we can—what's that?—a sharp report and a heavy blow, as if some gigantic fist has hit us. We know at once—it is the decisive moment! (See sketch at chapter heading.)

One second—two seconds—three seconds.

.   .   .   .   .

The seconds drip away into the past like sluggish oil. . . . Timidly, at first, and then with an ever-increasing rush comes the recognition of our inconceivable luck. We are not falling; we are still gliding. The two propeller blades only brushed past us when they broke away. Moreover, they both flew off at the same moment, so the engine still remains firmly embedded in its block.

Of the long blades only two short stumps remain. The air-pressure cannot move them—the engine is dead—and so, at last, at last the machine-gun is silenced.

A fine jet of water spurts over us. A splinter of wood has slit the cold-water jacket. What does it matter? The worst danger is over—we have liberty of action again.

I nod joyfully in the mirror to the good Roth, and he laughs joyfully back at me. Now our only job is to bring the propellerless machine safely down to earth. Already we have sunk below the ridges of the mountains which flank the Vardar valley. Obliquely, below us, our aerodrome beckons. Shall we be able to reach it in a prolonged glide, or must we make a forced landing outside? That would certainly be a bad business, because landing places are few and far between here in Macedonia.

Now we are only thirty metres above the lowest level of the valley—a flat turn to bring our nose into the wind—we flatten out—come to earth—taxi and come to a standstill, cleanly, on both wheels, with our tail-skid in the very middle of the aerodrome. Roth has made a masterly landing. (Photograph 1.)

We clamber out joyfully, and the first thing we do is to light cigarettes. Now all is well with us again.

Dear earth! Dear sun! Dear life!

And now our comrades come running up. Victims of such misfortunes are certain of a ragging. As we have come out of the business unscathed, hearts are eased and tongues loosened. The captain's relief twinkles visibly in the eye, unadorned by the monocle.

"Now, look here, my dear fellow! I fetch you from the West as an ace who can show my gentlemen what flying is, and then you let me down like that!"

But an impertinent greenhorn hands me a thin mulberry branch and declaims:

" Who is the greatest victor ?   He who conquers himself !

" Who is the greatest airman ?   He who shoots himself down ! "

We join in the laughter heartily.   Our lives are worth more to us than the price of a few jokes at our expense.

In the afternoon the machine is made serviceable again with a new propeller.   This time everything goes off according to plan.   The film-strips I bring home are good.

.   .   .   .   .

Bad news arrived from my old section.   Another two machines had been lost in the last month.   One was flown by Diessner, who was to have been my pilot after Engmann's death.   But we also had our own losses ; a reconnaissance machine, belonging to our forward Staffel at Drama, failed to return.

As we learnt later, Captain G. W. Murlis Green shot holes in both its tanks over Likovan—i.e., twenty kilometres behind the lines—so that the engine went dead and our people were forced to land at Mekes.   Two days later an Englishman flew over our aerodrome at Hudova at a great height and dropped a note, to which a streamer was attached. It informed us that both pilot and observer were slightly wounded, but otherwise well, and made inquiries about certain airmen whom we had taken prisoners.

The inquiry was unnecessary, because we always performed this comradely service on principle.   But it sometimes happened that the streamer of such a message was caught by the wind and carried away into the mountains, where it was impossible to recover it.

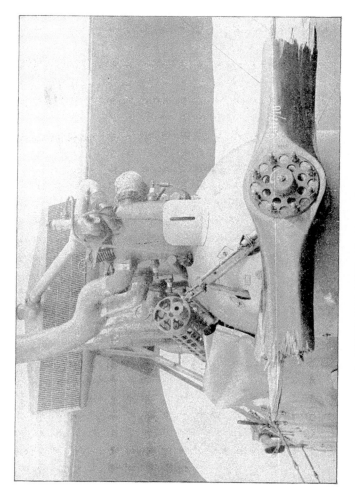

I. WHAT WAS LEFT OF THE PROPELLER

2. A MOTORING ROAD IN MACEDONIA

As there was a war on, it was not possible to eliminate the tragic incidents which disturbed these humane contacts every now and then. Thus, a machine belonging to a neighbouring section failed to return from a front patrol, and two English machines were reported flying over our aerodrome the following day. Lieutenant Burckhardt went up and shot one of them down.

With the dead pilot we found the note which he was to drop down ; it contained the news that both our people were prisoners but unwounded. Despite our joy at a victory we were very sorry for what had happened, but we could not possibly guess the nature of the mission on which the two English machines had set out.

My turn to-day—yours to-morrow !

As officer for serial photography, I had to instruct Lieutenant Gerth, who always brought some excellent pictures home. Unfortunately, I had to suspend his education because he and his pilot, Corporal Bruckhaus, were shot down and taken prisoners. Bruckhaus, an experienced pilot with many front patrols to his name, usually flew with Lieutenant Gessner, who had been sent elsewhere on temporary duty. Only a few weeks previously this couple had carried out a magnificent long-distance reconnaissance, which took them a great distance into Greece.

Happily, our scouts evened matters up the same day by bringing a two-engine Caudron down. It fell just behind the enemy's front line, where it was shot to pieces by Bulgarian batteries.

·   ·   ·   ·   ·

Now and then we had some very thick air of a night. Once my batman thumped me out of my sleep in pitch darkness.

B

" Two Farmans, 200 metres up, heading for drome ! "

A bomb raid ! But am I going to leave my warm bed and creep into the cold cellar ? Not likely ! Not every bomb hits its mark.

I listen excitedly. The roar of the engines sounds damned near. Hadn't I better . . . ? There it is —a " S-s-s-t," swelling in tones that grow ever higher, and then a dull " Humm! "

The earth shivers, and I hear a low crackling in the wall. I hold my breath—but the expected detonation does not come. A dud !

A few seconds later the performance is repeated, but in somewhat fainter tones : " S—t—Hum ! "

So that is another dud ! Then the roar of the engines dies away, and I fall asleep again. . . .

The next morning I had a look at the bombs. I did not need to go far, because the first dud—a 60-kilo bomb—lay only five metres from the corner of the hut where my bed stood. After removing all the glass from the windows of our airmen's castle and striking the neighbouring tent-hangar, we exploded the bomb.

The detonation was something to hear. Although, as careful folk, we dug a shallow crater round the bomb, the air-pressure was powerful enough to lift the roof off our dark room. If the heavy thing had gone off when it hit the ground, with me only five metres away behind my mud wall, I imagine that I should not have been particularly happy.

CHAPTER II

LIEUTENANT BRAUNECK—he fell after his ninth victory—shot down the leader's machine of an English squadron. It contained Major Black, the commander of No. 47 Squadron.

Accompanied by Hesse, who afterwards made a name for himself by his Berlin to Baghdad flight, I went to the scene of the crash to recover the body. We did not get back to Hudova until after midnight, because the roads were so damaged by the rainy weather that on one occasion it took a team of six horses to pull our car out of a mud hole.   (Photograph 2.)

As I was dead tired with the exertions of the journey, I intended to sleep late the following morning. But someone banged at my door in the grey dawn. Enemy aircraft again ?   No, it was only the skipper.

" Hearty congratulations !   You're taking over our Staffel at Drama.   Off to Greece with you ! "

.   .   .   .   .

The next day I took the train to Uskub, where I reported to Captain von Blomberg, the O.C. Aviation. Lieutenants Walter and Rittau initiated me into my job with the map.

" Your Staffel flies for the 20th Turkish Corps and the 10th Bulgarian division, with staff headquarters at Drama.   Here is your aerodrome, close to the town."

Walter passed his hand over several thousand square kilometres.   " Your reconnaissance area ! "

I measured the front.   From Orljak to the mouth of the Struma we had an air line of about sixty kilometres long overland ;   then came the coastal sector of about 100 kilometres from Rendina to the mouth of the Mesta.   I nodded.

" Altogether 160 kilometres of front for three reconnaissance machines ;   a bit of a tall order ! "

Rittau laughed.   " Can't be helped.   No more available.   But you've got a scout machine as well."

I pointed to the map.   " Three English aerodromes on the land front, and another two on the coast.   And we have one scout."

Then Rittau laughed again.   " Yes, but the scout is Eschwege ! "

.   .   .   .   .

I caught the train and resumed my journey.   It took me one day to reach Sofia, from which town I

needed a night, a day and another night to get to
Drama *via* Adrianople, Ferejik and Xanthi. I occupied a compartment with three Bulgarian officers, a
maior (major), a kapitan (captain), and a podporud-
schik (lieutenant), who shared their bread and local
wine with me in good comradely fashion. Each of
us occupied a corner, but they gave me a window
seat, so that they could show me their native land
better. When night fell, the three took one side of
the carriage to let me stretch myself out and sleep on
the other. I made a shamed protest against this act
of warm comradeship, but the major raised his hand
in a playful threat :

" You longer journey ! You leftnat, obey when
major command ! " They beamed when I told them
I was bound for Drama : " Ah—to Eschwege ! "

And they told me a few things about him. A few
days previously the Bulgarian official communiqué
had announced his fourth victory. (Photograph 3.)
The Bulgarian captain had been an eye-witness of his
second, and described it to me in detail.

" Eschwege—bjelomorssko orel, the Eagle of the
Aegean Sea ! "

The name stuck to him.

.   .   .   .   .

The English report on the operations of the 16th
Wing gave the following account of Eschwege's
fourth victory :

" On the morning of February 12th, 1917,
Captain Green and Lieutenant J. C. F. Owen took
off from Orljak aerodrôme, on their B.E.12s, to
attack and destroy the enemy Fokker scout of
Drama aerodrome. When our pilots had reached
the height of 6,300 feet, they saw the Fokker

climbing towards them. They immediately dived
on him and attacked him at a height of 5,400 feet
at a distance of forty-five feet. Unfortunately,
Captain Green's gun jammed. While he was clearing
the stoppage, Lieutenant Owen fought the Fokker
down to 1,800 feet, but probably either his engine
or his tank was hit, so that he was forced to land
in the vicinity of Drama aerodrome. When the
Fokker landed close beside him, the German pilot
sprang out and ran towards Lieutenant Owen, but
suddenly pulled up short—apparently he was afraid
of Lieutenant Owen's automatic pistol. Lieutenant
Owen set fire to his machine, which went up in
flames at once and was completely destroyed."

.   .   .   .

Shortly before midnight we crossed the former
Bulgarian frontier—we were in Greece. The train
ran into Drama in the early dawn. Behind the towers
of the churches and the minarets of the mosques rose
up mountains, which were overhung with grey
clouds. No flying weather !

Lieutenant Geisler, the former Staffel-leader, beamed
with the joy of leave, for on the morrow he was due
off for several weeks at home. Gradually the other
officers made their appearance, the last of them being
Lieutenant von Eschwege. He came from the
aerodrome, where he had been at work on his engine.
He was of medium height and almost delicate build.
Two blue eyes shone from his sharply-cut face.

" I'm sorry I can't offer you my hand," he said
with a smile, and held it out. It was as black as a
locksmith's. His tunic and trousers were covered
with oil smears.

After he had retired to his room to wash, the

others told me something about him. That was just
like him, they said. He loved his machine tenderly.
Even in wet weather he spent the whole day on the
aerodrome. After landing, it was seldom that he
would allow his mechanics to attend to his machine
unless he was with them. If his engine needed
overhauling, he worked late into the night with his
men. (See sketch at chapter heading.) How often
I saw him later sitting up by the engine in his overalls !

When he returned after a brief interval, I congratulated him on his fourth victory.

" It was a pity the other Englishman bolted so
quickly that I couldn't catch him up. It was a simpler
job with my third. He seemed to be a greenhorn.
He wasn't looking out, and so he let me come up
unseen to within a hundred metres of him—and
naturally that finished him."

" Boelcke says, too, that the approach is the main
thing."

" He's right, he's right ! If anyone asks me how I
do it—whether by flying or shooting—I say : ' Neither
one nor the other ! Just by approaching him ! '
Flying and shooting are part of the job ; naturally,
you've got to be all right in those matters. But the
approach is the chief thing. On principle I only
shoot when I'm within a hundred metres. And then
the other machine has to fall ! "

" Provided your gun doesn't jam ! "

" Of course, if the pilot takes no trouble about his
gun, if as soon as he lands, he thinks : ' Well, I can
retire into private life now that my flight is over,'
well, of course, it's no wonder that his gun jams."

" Yes, but have you never had a jam ? Often
the cartridges don't lie smoothly in the belt ; isn't
that so ? "

" I always fill my belts myself."

A sudden recollection made him laugh. " Once upon a time I didn't take so much trouble about my guns, either. But one learns wisdom through suffering. I'll have to tell you about that later, but now I should like to go off to the drome again, because I want to try out a small improvement with my men."

Lieutenant Geisler nodded to me. " We'll go along, too, and then I'll show you everything out there at the same time."

The more I saw, the more I realized how lucky I was to be put in charge of this Staffel. The first impression was good—and it lived up to its promise.

.   .   .   .   .

As soon as Geisler left, I took over. While we were sitting at lunch on the day after his departure, Eschwege suddenly whirled up from his seat and jerked the window open. His finely-tuned ears had registered the right impression, for the drone of an engine came down to us from a great height. He shook his head in amazement.

" I can't understand it ! The sky is so heavy with clouds that the Tommies can only see our Drama every now and then through a veil. No chance of observations or photography. The only possible thing they could do is to greet the new Staffel-leader by dropping a couple of little bombs in his soup."

We strained our ears to listen for anything that might come whistling down—and then felt somewhat relieved when the drone developed a deeper note after a few minutes. HE was flying away again. So we fed on in peace. But before I rose to terminate the session, the works sergeant entered with a bag attached to a streamer, which had been dropped over the aerodrome. I translated the enclosed letter :

To The
Commanding Officer
Aerodrome
DRAMA

In accordance with the usual custom carried out by both sides, we trust you will inform us of the fate of Lieutenant Swen who landed close to your aerodrome on February 18th.

I turned to Eschwege. " Your victim ? "

" No, unfortunately not ! That Tommy made a forced landing near Philippi on account of engine

trouble. Anyhow, we promptly dropped down the
news the next day from over Orljak, telling them not a
hair of his head was hurt. Probably the English
didn't see our streamer because their funk of our
bombs sent them into the cellar. By the way, that
good lad put his B.E. down very neatly. The
Bulgarians dismantled the bus at once and packed it
off to Sofia."

.   .   .   .   .

From the very beginning my activities in Drama
were under a lucky star. The cloud ceiling remained
closed for a few more days, so that I could work myself
into the job without disturbance and make contact
with my officers and men.

On February 27th Eschwege celebrated his twenty-
second birthday. It was a matter of course for him
to narrate some details of his career on this occasion.
The external facts were simple enough : ensign in the
Third Mounted Jaegers—August, 1914, sent from the
War Academy to join his regiment on active service
—February, 1915, sent home to a flying school—
five months later back at the front as a two-seater
pilot.

" I was within a hair's breadth of being returned
to my regiment for absolute incompetence because
I made quite a number of clean fractures. I flew my
two-seater for ten months at the front; then I was
allowed to train for a scout. That was May, 1916."

" And promptly shot your first down ? "

Eschwege made a gesture. " Ah, that was a
troublesome business. Nothing went right at first.
Now I know the cause ; it was only because I didn't
get close enough up to them. I was flying on the
Monastir front at the time, and once I caught a solitary

Farman. I put in a good burst and made him land with a damaged engine, but unfortunately on the other side of the lines. Naturally, my claim was not allowed. I wasn't at all sore about that.

"But I was furious about number two. I had joined our Staffel by then, and we were stationed at Xanthi. Once I managed to cut off a Farman from an English squadron at Thasos, which bombed our railway station. I had to give him nearly five hundred rounds before I shot his engine to pieces and forced him to glide down into the sea. Being a land machine, with wheels, it turned turtle at once and sank. When I landed again, a report from the Bulgarian observation post at the Mesta mouth sent in a report : 'Farman fell into the sea after fight with German machine.' I was blissfully happy because I naturally thought : 'Now you've got your first credited victory.' But that first victory is as hard to get as your first million marks. Unfortunately, it was a wash-out for me that time. You know how painfully exact the Kogenluft[1] is. 'Forward sworn statements of witnesses,' was the wire I got from him, but unluckily for me the Bulgarian regiment to which the observation post belonged had meanwhile been transferred to the Monastir front. We couldn't run down the witnesses.

"Two months later I brought an Englishman down over Drama. When he happened to mention a comrade who was shot down over Thasos in August and fell into the sea, we made another effort to find the observation post which had disappeared without leaving a trace, but, unfortunately, we couldn't locate them. That finished the business."

[1]Kogenluft = Kommandierender General der Luftstreitkräfte (General commanding the Air Forces).

" Yes, and when did you get your first credited victory ? "

Eschwege led me into his room and pointed to an aileron piece which he had nailed over the door.

" That's him ! Moreover, he's the chap I was wanting to tell you about—the schoolmaster who taught me to avoid unnecessary gun jams. The Bulgarians had started their advance into Greek territory while we remained at our old aerodrome at Xanthi. We were unable to carry out our aerial protection jobs properly because the new telephone connections were not working. So the English grew most impudent.

" I therefore fixed up a forward landing ground at Drama, and, lo and behold, an Englishman buzzed over it one fine morning at a low height and peppered the Bulgarians with his machine-gun when they were drilling. The moment he flew over my landing ground I took off. He flew so low that the houses masked him a few seconds later, and I had to drop down almost immediately after my start so as to avoid overclimbing him. The observer was so keen on his ground target that I took him completely by surprise. The first burst hit his machine, but then came my bad luck—a gun jam ! I was furious, because the pilot sheered off towards the lines at once. My best chance of success lay in a surprise attack, and that was gone ! (See illustration on jacket.)

" Yes, if only I had put a good burst into his machine at a hundred metres distance ! But now the observer slewed his gun round and opened fire on me. I went into a turn and shook my gun. When it was working again, I dived on him once more. This time the approach was not so comfortable, because the observer shot off a whole drum at me, and I had to fly right into his whizzing burst.

" Tacktacktack ! Three shots—then my gun jammed again. I believe I went as white as a ghost with the disappointment. I got out of his fire with another turn and then attacked him again. Two, three shots—gun jammed ! I began to think about beating a retreat and then I just imagined how those Tommies would split themselves with laughter when they landed ! I got into such a rage that I would have liked to ram their machine, even if I had to crash with it.

" So I tried again ! That time I got five shots out. And in that way I actually attacked them twenty-three times. Each time I just managed to put a few shots into their machine, but at last I did the trick. I shot up their engine and forced them to land this side of the lines. (Photograph 4.)

" That's why my first victory has always remained my favourite one. If I had killed the observer and then finished off the pilot without any danger to myself, I shouldn't have been satisfied. But that was really a first-class bit of work ; besides, it was the first machine to be shot down this side of the lines in our army's sector. The whole town rolled up in its excitement and gave me a heap of ovations."

Eschwege laughed cheerily. " When I think of my number two—he was really child's play ! Just fancy—two Serbian sergeants were ordered to fly a Farman from their aerodrome at Florina to Salonica— just a mild jaunt, you'd call it. But they lost their way and flew over Drama. ' Aha,' they thought, '*engelski aerodrom* (English aerodrome) ; we can go down and find out where we are ! But when they tried to put their Farman down, the guns opened on them. 'Oho,' says the man in charge, ' *kriwo adressirano* (we've come to the wrong address)' and opens out, with the idea of making himself scarce. But meanwhile I had climbed up and put a few bullets in his machine. So he accepted my invitation without further fuss and made a neat landing on our drome. (Photograph 5.)

"Our people killed themselves with laughing. I made those two chappies climb out, had a look at their machine and then took a little turn round the aerodrome in it. It behaved perfectly!"

CHAPTER III

I WAS sitting in the office when Eschwege entered. "Did Eckardt and Wethekam sight any English aircraft over the front?" he inquired.

"Not back yet."

He pulled out his watch. "They took off just after eleven, and it's now five past two. So they must be back soon! Well, I keep on going out so that I can catch them when they land and ask what's happening in the air over the lines."

. . . . .

A quarter of an hour later I rang up the aerodrome with some concern.

" Our machine not back yet ? "

" No, sir."

" How much petrol did it take ? "

" Main and gravity tanks both full."

I hung up the receiver. As the petrol would keep them in the air for three and a half hours, it meant that something must have happened if they did not return by 2.40 p.m. My anxiety drove me from the room.

" I shall be at the aerodrome if any news comes through," I announced.

Then I went off. I listened anxiously ; no sound in the air. I looked at the time ;   2.45 p.m. ; so they were overdue. Had they been shot down or had they made a forced landing somewhere ? If they had landed in the mountains, it meant waiting a long time for news, and if the worst had happened, it might be days before we heard anything about it. Hours of torturing suspense lay before me. I rang up the exchange.

" Tell Angeloff to ask the Bulgarian observation posts whether they can give us any information about our machine," I suggested.

Eschwege came across the aerodrome as I emerged from the tent.

" Any news ? " he asked.

I could only shake my head.

" What was their job ? " he inquired.

" Oh, quite a small business, just behind the lines —photos of the English camp at Orljak."

Then the telephone rang, and soon afterwards Angeloff transmitted the report of a Turkish observation post.

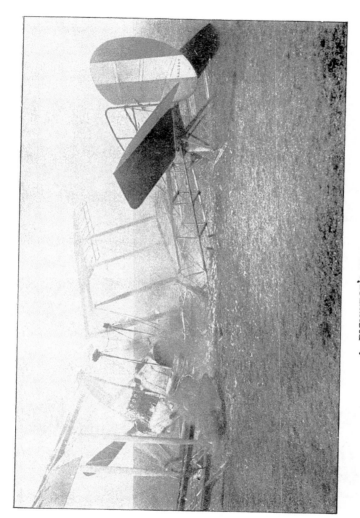

3. ESCHWEGE'S FOURTH VICTORY

4. ESCHWEGE'S FIRST VICTORY

5. ESCHWEGE'S SECOND VICTORY

" Two machines had a fight this morning. Then
both flew towards the mountains behind our lines
and disappeared from view. Some time afterwards
the English machine returned and landed at Orljak
aerodrome."

My fears grew. Our comrades must be lying
somewhere in the mountains, I thought . . . perhaps
dead, perhaps severely wounded. But we had no
notion of their whereabouts and could not help
them. But I took the precaution to ring up the
Turkish Headquarters in Radulevo and asked Captain
von Bardeleben, our liaison officer, to get inquiries
made.

Everyone was in low spirits at our gathering for
the afternoon tea which was usually such a cheery
affair. Hardly a word was spoken. The horrible
suspense was too much for us ! And it was so
difficult to get news, because we Germans could
only communicate with the Turks through a Bulgarian
exchange.

.   .   .   .   .

What had happened to our machine ?

Eckardt and Wethekam take off shortly after 11 a.m.

They cross the front at a height of 3,500 metres.
When Eckardt leans over to take his photographs,
Wethekam points downward to draw his attention to
an English B.E., which is screwing itself aloft, over
Dimitritch. Eckardt waves it aside disdainfully, as
if to say he will be through with his photography
before it is anywhere near.

He carries on. Ten minutes later the camp is on
his plates. He bends over joyfully to Wethekam and
whacks " Home ! " on his shoulder.

Wethekam has kept his eye on the Englishman all
the time. Now he puts his Albatros into a steep

c

right-hand turn in order to make his course for Drama. Eckardt stows away his camera and peers out in search of the Englishman.

A scout ! And already within a thousand metres distance. Eckardt releases the butt of his machine-gun and rattles off a few bullets in his direction. " We have spotted you, old friend," they say. " You needn't think you can surprise us ! "

Uninfluenced, however, by this message, the B.E. continues to approach, flying at the same level as the Albatros. When the English pilot is within a hundred metres, he pushes his stick down and hangs on underneath the tail of the German machine, where no bullet can reach him. Just as Eckardt bends over to whack Wethekam into a turn, the first burst rattles up at him. He feels something strike him hard on his head. The next moment blood pours down over his eyes. A bullet has passed through his right cheek bone, damaging the eye, and then emerging through the frontal bone. (See sketch at chapter heading.)

Luckily, the B.E. pilot has fired all the twenty-five rounds of his drum and goes into a turn to change it. Wethekam sees him turn out from under the cockpit and wonders why his observer does not open fire. The Englishman presents an excellent mark now !

A backward glance gives him the answer. Lieu-tenant Eckardt is sitting on his tip-up seat, with blood pouring from him. He has torn off his helmet and goggles, and is putting a bandage on the wound.

At once Wethekam sees the danger which threatens them both. His observer cannot fire another shot, and this old machine carries no forward gun, so that he cannot attack the enemy himself. A downward glance. They have crossed the trenches in the Struma

plain and are approaching the mountains, where a
landing may mean death. But better this possible
end than the certain death to which the Englishman
will send him down! The only hope of salvation
is to go down and land! Perhaps the B.E. may
funk following him down to a low height amid the
mountain peaks.

But, meanwhile, the speedier opponent has changed
his drum and is once more hanging on underneath
his tail. The "tacktacktacktacktack" rattles up to
his ears again.

Wethekam strives to wriggle out of the burst by a
series of crazy turns. With his engine full on he
pushes the stick down until his bracing wires scream
as they cleave the air. But the Englishman has
noticed that he has put the German observer out of
action and is therefore unwilling to let go the opportunity to shoot the machine down without risk to
himself.

He hangs on. In a little while he gives his gun its
third drum and rattles out a new burst which is more
accurate than the second one. With dismay Wethekam hears bullets hitting the engine. His rev-
counter drops—the propeller flutters round a few
more times—then it goes dead. That is the end!

They are only a few hundred metres above the
ridge of the mountain range. It is high time to
look about for a spot where the machine can be put
down. But no landing place is visible; far and wide
there is nothing to be seen but ridges and precipices
and steep cliffs. Where are they going to crash?

The machine with the dead propeller glides lower
and lower. Wethekam wants to put it into one more
right-hand turn to see what the Englishman is doing.
Slowly he applies his lateral controls, but what has

happened? The rudder-bar gives no resistance to his foot—a bullet has shot its wire away. That is bad enough, but at a pinch he can get round on his ailerons.

Wethekam pushes his stick across, but there is no response—not even when he uses his body-weight most energetically. The wire which has been shot away has jammed the aileron controls.

The unsteered machine glides down towards the wall of rock. Wethekam can control nothing but his elevator. But what use is that to him when his engine is out of action? Now he cannot bring the machine past the mountains, which seem to loom larger before him every second. Only one faint consolation remains to him—the Englishman has turned back. If he had realized the helpless state of the German machine and attacked it just once more, it would have been easy enough for him to give the *coup de grâce*.

Deeper and deeper they glide. By pulling his stick Wethekam strives to prolong the glide and so clear the mountain ridge in order to go down in the valley beyond it. In vain! As soon as he puts the machine's nose up too much, it stalls and threatens to go into a sideslip. That would be even worse than running into the wall of rock. So he must put the stick down again to gain new way on the machine.

The rocky wall rises up sheer before him a few hundred metres away. Will he be able to bring the machine down on its ridge? If he pancakes her a bit hard, he will probably crack off the undercarriage, and then they will stop up there.

The wheels are touching the rock—then—new terrors come into sight. The mountain ridge is quite a narrow one, and behind it opens out a rocky valley—sloping downward for hundreds of metres. If he puts the machine down here, they will taxi over the edge into this ravine, and then they are finished.

Instinctively Wethekam pulls the stick up against his chest. The wheels have already touched the ground, but the rubber springs on the axle of the undercarriage bounce them up again ; the machine begins to stall and tries to sideslip. Stick down ! The wounded bird droops her head and glides over the precipice into the valley beyond.

What have they gained by that ? Their doom is postponed for a minute or so, but it certainly awaits them down yonder between the masses of rock with which the gorge is strewn. Yes, if only Wethekam could use his lateral controls, he might be able to put the machine down on a tolerably smooth patch of ground. But the controls are shot away ! He has no alternative but to land just where he happens to come down.

Walls of rock that might have been built by some spectral hand tower up to heaven—near and nearer to the ground drops the machine—and then—Wethekam's eyes gleam with joy—they are heading for a gentle rise. What matters it that this slope is strewn with stones and scree—it greets the unsteered craft like a port on a storm-tossed sea. Let the machine smash up if it will, the main thing is to land it with the dangerously wounded observer inside—and land it so that it comes down between the rocks with the least possible way on it.

As Wethekam flattens out, he perceives with horror that the wind is pushing him to one side. Now the right wheel touches the ground—but at the same moment the right wing bangs against a rock—breaks

—and then the machine splinters as it crashes against the ground. (Photograph 6.)

.   .   .   .   .

Wethekam crawls out laboriously from the debris. Thank heaven ! They were mercifully preserved. His only visible injury seemed to be a gash under his right eye. And then he found he could not use his right foot very well ; the ankle seemed to be sprained. He hobbled wearily round the machine, looking for Lieutenant Eckardt, who lay wedged between the ruins. After extracting him carefully from under bent metal and splintered wood, he bandaged his wounds anew.

What next ? His eye fell on the chronometer, which hung in a rubber case and was therefore still working, despite the fearful crash. 1.1 p.m. His decision was quickly made.

" I'll go down the valley to the nearest village where troops are quartered. There I can get on the phone to Drama and ask them to fetch us."

After a two hours' tramp he reached Dovishta, where a Turkish regiment lay in peaceful quarters. He only hoped he could make himself understood by them !

When the Turks recognized him as a German by his uniform, they took him to their regimental commander. Wethekam tried to tell him what had happened by waving his arms to illustrate his broken French :

" Aleman aeroplan kaputt ! "

The Turkish officer shook his hand warmly and answered in the purest Saxon :

" Well, then you're a lucky fellow ! "

(" I was flabbergasted," said Wethekam, when he subsequently told me his stôry of the meeting. " A small, insignificant Turk, and he spoke very good German.")

The officer was Lieutenant-Colonel Schierholz, of the 107th Regiment at Leipzig, who went to Turkey in 1913 with the German military mission. He proved to be an active helper, for he quickly drew up a report of the affair, which he pressed into the hands of a Jewish interpreter for despatch to Drama. Then Wethekam went back to the scene of the crash with a party of soldiers, after which two men took the wounded observer to the hospital at Dovishta, where an Austrian medical officer in Turkish service gave his wounds the first skilled attention.

. . . . .

Meanwhile I waited in Drama for news. The suspense was terrible, but—at last, at last !—Wethekam's telephone message reached me late in the evening. We breathed freely again. Our men were alive—at last I had definite news, at last I could do something !

" The large car to be at the officers' mess at 5.30 a.m. to-morrow with Dr. Woermann and Lieutenant Kuhlo," I ordered.

. . . . .

We started off in the grey dawn, without waiting for Kuhlo, who had misunderstood the time. However, he quickly borrowed a little blood-stock mount from our friend, Fuad Bey, and overtook us at Tapol monastery about noon. I sent him on in advance, to make contact with the Turks.

Travelling via Zelaova, we did not reach Dovishta until about 4 p.m. Although it was only thirty kilometres from Drama as the crow flies—we could fly the stretch in ten minutes—our best car needed a good ten hours for the journey.

To our great joy we found Eckardt doing as well as could be expected, with a good doctor to look after him. So now, to have a look at the machine ! But Lieutenant-Colonel Schierholz held me back.

" I'll give you some mountain ponies and a guide. You'd better have some refreshment while you're waiting for them."

A few minutes later we were sitting down to scrambled eggs and maize bread, but, unfortunately, the good wishes for the future of our dear Schierholz Bey (which we expressed as thanks for his hospitable comradeship) were not fulfilled. He was carried off by fever on the Palestine front six months later.

After our meal we mounted and rode off into the mountains, following the course of the Kakara stream along narrow bridle-paths. After two hours of it I asked our guide whether we were likely to arrive soon.

" Ewe, efendim," he replied, and wagged his head in confirmation. At the next bend of the way he pointed down the valley to where a broken wing rose up out of the wreckage, while Turkish soldiers squatted round a fire in front of their tents. Carefully feeling the way with their front hoofs, our ponies climbed up between rocks and scree to the floor of the valley. We dismounted and climbed a small slope to reach the machine.

It was a scene of desolate heaps of wreckage. Wethekam pointed up to the wall of the mountain that stood out dark against the evening sky. Up there was the spot where he first put his machine down yesterday morning, but then pulled it up again to land in the valley after a long glide. I looked into his eyes and pressed his hand gladly and gratefully.

6. AFTER THE FRAY

7. (Left to Right) DR. WOERMANN, ECKARDT, GREIFF

8. THE SILVER-GREY NIEUPORT

9. ENGINE AND MACHINE GUN OF THE SOPWITH TWO-SEATER WHICH CRASHED IN THE MOUNTAINS

Suddenly we pricked up our ears in amazement. The drone of an engine ! Soon afterwards we saw an English machine, flying from the direction of the front, swing into our valley. Having learnt that an airman had previously circled round the spot at a low height during the morning and located the landing place, we could only conclude that this one was going to bomb the remains of the Albatros. I ordered everyone to take cover, so as to make his task more difficult. The machine circled round at some distance away and then flew off—its inmates had been unable to find our machine.

We reached Dovishta again in the evening. I rang up for four men from the Staffel to come along and then left Kuhlo to direct the salvage operations.

We others returned to Drama by train, arriving in the twilight of the next morning.

Eckardt was very silent. The doctor's verdict was that he must not only lose his right eye, but that the left one was also in danger. I therefore sent him off from Drama to the Alexander Hospital at Sofia to see a specialist. (Photograph 7.)

We waited anxiously for further news. And then came the joyful tidings that his left eye was saved.

. . . . .

The machine and its crew would have been lost if Lance-Corporal Wethekam had not kept his head and piloted it skilfully into the valley. I therefore wired a request for his promotion, and received a quick answer :

" Express my appreciation of pilot Wethekam's gallant flight and promote him corporal for distinguished service as from March 12th, 1917. Kofl 11—bejovk—von Below."

And then came another telegram :

" Express my appreciation of the valiant Lieutenant Eckardt and his pilot. Hope they will soon
have their revenge, nr. 205, commanding officer
of the 20th tverk a.k. General Abdul Kerim."

Eckardt was too badly wounded ; he could not
secure compensation himself. But mindful of our
Staffel's principle, " One for all and all for one,"
Eschwege obtained it for him.

Two days later he had a fight with two English
machines and forced one of them to land at Doksat.
Both its inmates were badly wounded. Lieutenant
Sidney Beare (R.N.A.S.), the pilot, had a flesh wound
in his head, and another bullet passed through his
foot, while Lieutenant Edgar Percy Hyde (R.F.C.),
the observer, had five bullet wounds in his legs and
buttocks. Nevertheless, they succeeded in firing
their machine before the Bulgarian soldiers arrived.
(Photograph 8.)

I should have liked to capture their silver-grey
Nieuport intact, but could only admire the pluck of
those two gallant lads.

.   .   .   .   .

And a week later another English machine went
down—a Sopwith two-seater this time. Here is
Eschwege's combat report :

REPORT.

" On 30.3.17 I took off at 10.15 a.m. from my
forward landing ground and flew to Sarishaban to
attack an enemy aircraft proceeding from Thasos
in the direction of Xanthi. I came up with this
machine, a Sopwith biplane, about 60 kilometres
north of Xanthi and fired about 50 rounds into it at
a distance of 80 metres. The enemy aircraft

immediately went into a steep left-hand turn and did not return fire because, as was subsequently ascertained, one of my first shots disabled its machine-gun. I gave it another 40 rounds at 20 metres distance, whereupon it went down in a spin, in the course of which I saw splinters detach themselves from the machine. I followed in a steep glide and saw the machine strike a sugar-loaf mountain with full force and break up.

LIEUTENANT VON ESCHWEGE."

The inmates, Lieutenants Ingham and Maxwell, both of the R.N.A.S., were dead. The machine was hurled against the rocks with such force that the barrel of the machine-gun and the push rods of the rotary engine were bent like wires. (Photograph 9.)

That was the retaliation for the wound inflicted on our comrade Eckardt, and therewith Eschwege achieved his fifth and sixth credited victories.

CHAPTER IV

THE MARSH BIRDS

ESCHWEGE stood by his machine, running his engine, as I strolled out to the aerodrome.

" Where are you going to-day ? " I asked.

He placed his mouth to my ear in order to make himself understood above the roar of the engine. " To the Struma front ! The Thasos brethren can have a rest ! "

Up and down the lines flies Eschwege for a long time. Nothing in sight. What a pity ! Petrol is running out, and so he must go home, however distasteful the compulsion may be.

But stay—white shrapnel cloudlets are developing in the air over Angista station! And down yonder great fountains of earth rise up—bomb-bursts! So, off to them!

But Eschwege searches the sky keenly. How many English machines are there? He must keep an eye on every one of them, if he does not want to have an invisible opponent sitting on his back.

Only two! Apparently 140 h.p. B.E.s, sturdy, nimble fellows—that may mean a hot fight. They increase in size rapidly as they approach out of the haze. Now they are only 1,000 metres away—in another ten seconds he will have joined issue with them.

Now he has got the right distance—a steep dive—then he pulls his machine up and puts a burst into the nearest of them from below. But while the machine he has attacked goes into a sharp turn in its endeavour to escape the shower of bullets, the other pilot slews round, and in the twinkling of an eye Eschwege is well in his burst. The thin threads of the tracer bullets shoot by him to right and left, and suddenly he hears a metallic thud in his engine—a hit! The next moment he feels two hard blows on his right arm—he is wounded!

He raises his arm. He can still move it—not so bad! But he has no time to worry about it, for the B.E. is sitting on his neck and following him in his turn.

Best way out—sideslip down! A hard tug at the stick—the Albatros shoots up so that the Englishman must push his machine away to avoid a collision—and then Eschwege slips down over the right wing.

He spins earthwards like a falling leaf. After dropping several hundred metres he catches his machine again and looks about him to locate the two Englishmen. They are flying towards Lake Takhino, behind which lies their forward landing ground at Monuhi. So after them !

But what's up ? The rev-counter is crawling back and the engine begins to sputter. A glance at the manometer. No more pressure on the main tank ! The engine is getting no more petrol and will go dead in a moment. Apparently there's something wrong with the automatic pump. Ah, yes—that metallic thud that he heard during the fight re-echoes in his ears—probably the bullet hit it. Then try the handpump ! A few energetic pushes—but the little hand of the pressure gauge refuses to move. So the bullet must have gone right through the main tank.

Doesn't matter ! The gravity tank contains petrol for another half-hour's work. Time enough to polish off one of the two and get home safely.

His hand goes to the switch—several seconds of suspense—then new fuel flows once more into the carburettor—and the slender hand of the rev-counter slides over slowly to the right, towards the 1,600.

A glance ahead. Aha! the two Englishmen are still there, but meanwhile they have gained more than a kilometre on him. He hopes he will catch them up in time, for obliquely below him he can see the mirror of the lake.

A few quick shots ! Too far to hit them, but just a message : " Here I am again ! "

And lo and behold ! The moment after they have heard the shots they turn round to resume the fight. They thought they had finished the German off when

they saw him go down in a spin, but there he is again
—asking for more—all right, he shall have it!

Fifteen seconds later machine-guns are rattling
away. The Bulgarian Archie gunners stand by their
telescope and shrug their shoulders. Nothing doing
for them; up there is a wild medley of machines:
turning, climbing, diving, so that it is impossible for
them to pick out cross from cockade.

But wait a moment—the mess is sorting itself out.
A machine is making for the farther shore in a steep
glide. A quick peep through the glasses reveals it
as an English one. The German is sitting on his
neck—he is Eschwege! It looks as if he has shot
up the enemy's engine and is now going to finish him
off.

But Eschwege could not finish him off, for the
comrade of his prospective victim came down on him
and forced him to turn away after a few shots. For a
while they went round and round in a hot battle of
turns, and then the second Englishman sheered off
and skimmed across the lake towards his landing
ground. Then Eschwege likewise turned away and
flew back to Drama.

.   .   .   .   .

I was waiting for him on the aerodrome, and
rejoiced at his neat landing. The propeller went dead
when he finished taxying. He turned the starter in
vain; the engine made no movement. He bade
Osterwald swing the propeller—in vain! He rose
from his seat dejectedly and soon found the solution
of the riddle. The gravity tank was empty; he had
flown to his last drop of petrol.

I knew no victory had come to him this flight as
soon as I saw his face.

" I had one of them dead in my sights," he said,
" and could not get him. And why not ? Because
the other gave him such splendid help. A great lad !
I'm certain he was Captain Green. If not, I'd have
got the other ; he seemed a greenhorn. But whenever I put my burst into him, the captain came and sat
on me."

He pulled off his leather jacket. " He holed my
main tank and gave my arm two nasty knocks, which
burnt like hell. But one thing I know for certain ;
I put a few nice hits into the greenhorn's machine.
Unfortunately, I couldn't attend to him any more
because the other fellow raked me so viciously. No
report there from the front ? I'd like to know what
happened to the little fellow ! "

I could only shrug my shoulders in sympathy.
Then we went off messwards in the dumps.

There was still no news when we were sitting over
our afternoon coffee. Eschwege grew nervous.

" It's disgusting !" he vowed. "I swear I shot his
engine up. I saw his prop go dead quite plainly.
If he managed to get past the marsh, I hope he
crashed his machine when he landed ! "

.   .   .   .   .

We sat over our evening meal in deep dejection,
chewing bread and dripping and the usual tomatoes.
Then the interpreter rushed in, beaming with joy.

" He fell in the marsh ! "

" Fire away, Angeloff, and tell the story from the
beginning ! "

" Telephone report from the Bulgarian Archies on
Lake Takhino : two English machines bombed
Angista station this morning. Then they had a fight
with a German airman, and then one Englishman

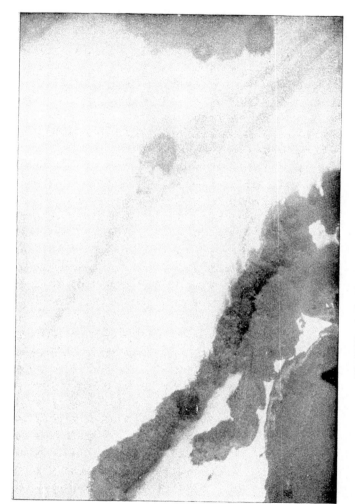

10. THE PATCH OF OIL ON LAKE TAKHINO

11. SALONICA HARBOUR FROM THE AIR

landed at Monuhi. The other was hit and could not reach the farther shore. Fell into the lake where it's marshy, about five hundred metres from Takhino village. Machine's there still, with its nose in the water and its tail sticking up."

While each of us in turn shook Eschwege's hand, Angeloff stood at attention. As soon as we were quiet again, he continued :

" This afternoon some English came in a boat and worked on the machine. Probably they took the pilot off. We think, perhaps, they'll come again to-morrow to salve the machine."

I gave Eschwege a laugh. " Perhaps not ! Supposing we two dropped a few bombs on it in the morning ! "

Eschwege was all for it.

. . . . .

We started at break of day the next morning, with a hundredweight of bombs on board. From a hundred metres up Eschwege put the stick down, and dived on to the dummy machine that served as our target in order to test his gun. My heartbeats increased as our bird dived down like a hawk swooping on a hare. All my hairs stood on end when I found Eschwege cutting things as fine with the heavy, bomb-laden two-seater as he did with his light scout, for I had a painful feeling that we were going to hit the ground the next moment, and, if so, we should have made a lovely crash when all our bombs went off. We descended until we almost touched the ground ; then our bird's head went up slightly. She hopped over the target with a bare margin and went into a steep climb.

We flew very low, because the winds were still

asleep and so we need expect no dangerous gusts.
We dropped still deeper when we were over the lake
and headed for the huts of Takhino village.

We peered ahead in search of our objective, until
at last Eschwege raised his arm, pointed to the right
and laughed at me.   Then I quickly caught sight of
the machine.   The Bulgarian gunners had observed
correctly ; it was sticking in the marshy water, nose
downwards.   We flew round the spot and had a look
at this bird from all sides.

Then I made Eschwege turn away and whacked
him on to the course.   Yes, now we were in the
right direction.   I gave him the signal, and he headed
for the target.   It loomed up at the side of my right
wing.

Bad flying !   Try again !   We went back in a
turn and headed for it anew.   Meanwhile I searched
the horizon for enemy aircraft—the sky was clear.
I felt at ease when I saw that both the tents at Monuhi
were closed.   The Englishmen were still asleep, so
that I could lay my eggs at ease.

After carefully whacking Eschwege on to the right
course, I bent overboard.   The target came up
quickly—we were dead on it.   I had calculated
correctly and dropped my four bombs at intervals of
a few seconds.   Then I whacked Eschwege's shoulder
joyfully :—banked turn so that we can watch results !

A few seconds of tension, and then—just my luck !
—two bombs burst in front of it and two behind !
Four brown cascades of mud rose up towards us and
then fell back into the marsh with a plomp.   As soon
as Eschwege had cut his engine, we sent a Red Indian
war-cry of triumph across to Monuhi aerodrome to
give vent to our unrestrainable joy.   Then, without
warning, Eschwege put the machine on to her nose,

so that I had to make a quick grab at the sides of the cockpit while he rattled a burst of a hundred shots into the target, after which I gave the debris of it a whole drum of 250 rounds. That was some shooting! The bullets sent the marsh water up in merry splashes as they struck home, giving us an ideal mark.

We flew home very happy.

·   ·   ·   ·   ·

Two days later our Bulgarian observation post reported that another boat worked its way through the mud to the crashed machine, but after a little while it returned. Probably they did no more than photograph the remains.

Moreover, we knew we had riddled the tanks, because the sluggish current of the lake forced the petrol out. The stream it formed was plainly visible.

Later the machine sank gradually into the marsh. (Photograph 10.)

·   ·   ·   ·   ·

Several months afterwards I was reminded of our raid when I cross-examined a captured Englishman. He told us that his people wanted to salve the remains of the machine, but found it so riddled by the bombs and machine-gun fire that it was no longer worth the trouble.

CHAPTER V

OUR FRIENDS THE ENGLISH

OUR friends the English !
With his awkward hand the Bulgarian N.C.O.
signed the following formula :

RECEIPT.

———

......shot down English aviator(s)
Name(s) ....

Received with thanks
Drama Aerodrome.............

Then he motioned to the two Voyniks, who waited
with fixed bayonets in front of the door of our mess.

" Good-bye, gentlemen ! " said the receipted one,
giving each of us in turn a hearty handshake.

Before he turned the corner with his Bulgarian
escort, he bestowed another friendly wave on us.   I
looked at Eschwege thoughtfully.   " Isn't it perfectly
swinish that we've got to fly against the Tommies ?
Just imagine what it would have been like if we had
been fighting on the same side, my lad ! "

" Yes, God knows," he replied.   " We've had a
lot of English airmen here already, and they were one
and all good fellows."

Lieutenant Lenz laughed.   " That I can well
imagine.   A Tommy in the hand is better than a
Tommy in the air."

But Eschwege did not fall in with his mood.
" Don't talk rot," he said.   " I'm dead serious.   I
can't help it, but I like them all.   Not only in the
mess ; I like them in the air as well, when it hasn't
been decided who's too rash.   And I'm very pleased
that they like us too."   He turned to me again.
" Before you came here, the English dropped a note
with the following contents :

" As we have met so often in the air and peppered
one another, we should also be very pleased to make

the personal acquaintance of the German airmen of
Drama. We therefore make the following proposi-
tion. Give us your word of honour that you will
not take us prisoners, and then we will land a
motor boat on the eastern shore of Lake Takhino
to meet you."

Unfortunately, we had bad experiences with that sort
of fraternization not long before on the Russian
Front, and so there was 'an order issued, forbidding
us to go in for anything of the kind—and I'm still
heartily sorry about it, for I should have been ever
so pleased to shake hands with those Tommies."

I nodded my approval. " Above all, I'm glad they
consider us as decent chaps as themselves."

Suddenly Eschwege gave vent to a loud laugh.
" That's not the end of the tale. When there was
nothing doing with the picnic idea, they wanted to
arrange a small sporting event with us, at least.
So, in all seriousness, they made a proposal for an
aerial battle over Lake Takhino. They were ready
to guarantee that their Archies would not shoot during
the meeting, and we were to vouch for the silence of
the Bulgarians. Just think of it—a squadron tourna-
ment in the air ! "

I grinned mirthfully. ' They would certainly
have won it, with their forty-eight machines to our
four. It would have meant twelve Englishmen
attacking each one of us."

Eschwege's face showed that he felt offended.
" Or each one of us would have attacked twelve
Englishmen," he corrected.

. . . . .

These apparently exaggerated figures were, unfortunately, only too accurate. No. 17 Squadron of

the R.F.C. opposed us on the Struma front, while a naval squadron, stationed at Thasos, was our adversary on the Aegean front.   As each squadron consisted of three flights of eight machines, we had to hold our own against forty-eignt machines with our four, which were increased to five later.

Luckily, they were unable to exploit the advantage of these heavy odds in the way one might have supposed, for in addition to having Rudi von Esch-wege on our side we could count on the assistance of two other allies—time and space.   Even with their four dozen machines, it was simply impossible for them to put an aerial barrage along fronts that measured sixy kilometres by land and one hundred by sea.   In addition to this we developed a marvellous luck.

Assuredly, not even a close reconnaisance was a joyride, for in spite of the heavy losses we inflicted on them, the English were a plucky crowd.   This fact was demonstrated to us in a most unpleasant fashion on the occasion of the long-distance recon-naissance to Salonica, which we undertook in combi-nation with the German sections 30 and 34 (Hudova Aerodrome), and the two Bulgarian *aeroplannoto otodelenie* 1 and 2 (Han Velica and Hudova Aero-dromes).   The best photograph was taken by Lieutenant Gessner, of No. 30.   (Photograph 11.)

Large depots had been formed in Salonica because all men and materials for the Entente's Balkan armies (consisting of English, French, Italian, Russian, Serbian, Venizelist-Greek, Indian, Algerian, Anna-mese and Senegalese troops) were landed at that port. The strength and number of these depots had to be checked at regular intervals in order to guard the Bulgarian G.H.Q. against any unpleasant surprises.

But negative as well as positive changes took place in Salonica.   On August 18th, 1917, the town was ravaged by a fire which assumed catastrophic dimensions when fanned by a stiff northerly breeze.   About 9,500 houses were burnt to ashes, while nearly 80,000 inhabitants were homeless, and the damage was estimated at something like 160 million marks.   The conflagration began in a wooden house in Olympus Street, which was set on fire by some oil that boiled over, but the Balkan gossip-mongers naturally had better information concerning its origin.   They asserted that the German airmen sprinkled the town with a white powder, which set it on fire.

The staff of the German Admiralty also laid great value on our reports.   They were mainly interested in the arrivals and departures of the ships which provided raw material for the work of our U-boats.

The regular appearance of our reconnaissance machines was a thorn in the eye of G.H.Q., Salonica, which went to considerable trouble to deal with the nuisance.   The tightening up of their well-organized intelligence system gave us a lot of work.   The enemy had established a number of observation posts all along the front, which reported us by wireless to his aerodromes as soon as any of our machines crossed the lines.   Their scouts promptly took off to find us ; when they were in the air, they were guided towards us by directional marks laid out on the ground.   Later on the indications were supplemented by figures, giving the number of German machines reported. (Photograph 12.)

．　　．　　．　　．　　．

We never grew tired of the pleasure of welcoming an Englishman as our guest.   But when one of them

—Lieutenant Leslie-Moore—expressed a wish for a cup of coffee after the meal, I had to confess to him that we had none and that he must make shift with tea.

" Oh," he said, " you have allowed me to write a note to the Major to say how I'm getting on, and you're going to drop it down.   So I'll ask him to send you some coffee.   That's all right ! "

He wrote the following letter :

Dear Major
        I have just
dinned with the German
Flying Corps. They
have been very kind
to me. I am going
up to Philopopolis
to-morrow. The Germans
have asked me to ask
you to throw them over
some Coffee which they
want in mess here
        Good luck to all,
                A Leslie- Moore

A few days after his letter had fluttered down the other side of the lines, an Englishman appeared at a respectful height over our lines. Unfortunately, we could not catch the streamer he dropped, because a strong wind carried it away into the mountains. But we were gratefully convinced that it contained the coffee we desired. I can only hope that it did not agree with the dishonourable finder.

.   .   .   .   .

To the honour of the English airmen I must admit that nearly all of them refused to give information on military matters. Once, when I tried to squeeze some out of a little lieutenant, he said with a smile :

" Dear commander, if you or any of your gentlemen were shot down by my friends, would you tell any tales ? "

I could only shrug my shoulders and smile too.

But despite my respect for the silence of our English comrades of the air, I could not do without their information. Our intelligence service tapped many sources, such as observations from the ground, aerial photography, intercepted wireless messages, captured papers, reports from secret agents, etc. The statements of our own people who escaped from captivity were particularly fruitful, and in this way we obtained valuable material from a Bulgarian sergeant, who had worked at Thasos aerodrome for a long time.

But the greatest pleasure of all was that which we derived from a man in rags, whom the Bulgarians had arrested as a spy somewhere round about the mouth of the Struma. He turned out to be Sergeant Scheede, of the 9th Jaegers, who commanded a working party of fifty German prisoners at the Salonica aviation park after having been captured at Monastir. He brought us a whole sackful of important news items, some of which enabled me to make many captive airmen talkative later on.

As we were at war, I had the habit of making a slight digression when my progress along the main road was blocked. I collected all the general information about the enemy and the special news about his aviation units; by balancing up reports which contradicted each other, I was able to gain a fairly clear picture of things. In this fashion I could bluff my prisoners in advance by my knowledge of men and affairs, for when the latter were forced to assume that I knew certain things (although very often my " knowledge " was just a bold deduction) they did not exercise sufficient care in their conversations with me.

One day, for instance, I exhibited our photographs of an English aerodrome to a prisoner, because I wanted to squeeze out of him information as to why their hangars had disappeared and been replaced by tents, when the contrary process was the usual one. Having planned my tactics in advance, I fired away at him :

" What do you think of the marvellous success of the raid the Bulgarians made on your aerodrome at Badimal ? "

He flared up at once. " That's an untrue report ! "

I laughed. " I must confess the direct hit on the hangar was a bit of luck, and I can quite understand that you don't admit its success. But I can prove it to you straight away ! "

Then I showed him our photographs in chronological order :

(1) A large hangar.
(2) The hangar has vanished.

(3) Two tents up in its place.

(4) Five tents up.

I grinned with the slyness of a peasant in order to provoke him. The result was that he flew into a temper at once.

" No, that's no proof ! " he vowed. " It was no bomb dropped by the Bulgarians that did the mischief, but a pure accident. When one of our airmen was returning from a raid on a place where the clouds covered his target, he was so over-conscientious that he brought his bombs home again. Unfortunately he made a bit of a rough landing, so that the things went off and blew him to pieces. They also wrecked the hangar and five other machines. The disappearance of the hangar has absolutely nothing to do with any Bulgarian raids."

I nodded thoughtfully and said to myself : " Many thanks for the kind information ! "

.   .   .   .   .

At 5 a.m. one morning my entire force assembled on the aerodrome—three pilots and three observers for the two-seaters, two pilots for the scout machines. Yes, that was the whole of my force. The orders were : " Bomb raid in squadron formation." In order to make it a really effective raid I had arranged for all the two-seaters to carry two hundredweight more of bombs than the regulations allowed. Even the two scouts had two $12\frac{1}{2}$ kilo eggs apiece. I had fixed upon Stavro harbour as our objective, because so much building had been going on there in the last few months—new piers, new sidings, and new sheds. (Photograph 13.)

.   .   .   .   .

I could not guess at the time that our frequent

raids on Stavro must be considered as most rude
ruthlessness by the Tommies.   This fact I learnt only
later from H. Collinson Owen's book, *Salonica and
After*, in which the author states :

" One of the most favoured spots in all Macedonia
was Stavro . . . a sweet little place of noble hills,
covered with dense olive-green scrub and trees, running down to the edge of a blue sea.

" The climate was generally beautiful, although
very hot and relaxing in summer, but there were
winter and spring and autumn days there that were
a dream of delight.

" There were only two drawbacks to life there, the
mosquitoes and the enemy aeroplanes, but these,
after all, were common to all the front.   But for the
bombs and the frequent rumble of the guns, it was
really possible to forget the war.   Sitting on a little
verandah, with the magnificent colours of evening
shining on the bay, it was as good as an evening in
Monaco, with the added charm of a picnic.   A
bright moon could be seen shining through the
trees, and the nightingales—hundreds of them
apparently—were so busy with their singing that it
was almost a clamour.

" Only the absence of Eve marred all such
gatherings.   There is no doubt about it that Stavro
was made for honeymoon couples, but alas ! there
were no honeymoons to be had in the B.S.F."

.   .   .   .   .

We started about 6 a.m.   With the heavy loads
we had taken, we were compelled to cross the front
at the Struma mouth at a fairly low height.   We were
thankful to find the anti-aircraft batteries shooting so
thoroughly badly that day that we crossed without

sustaining a single hit. There were no English aircraft to be seen.

We passed over Stavro in good squadron order and dropped our bombs on to the remunerative targets. Both the land batteries and the warships there made miserable shooting and failed to worry us; all our bombs, therefore, were well aimed. An hour and a half later, we all made good landings in Drama.

We had not long to wait for a most ample and massive return visit. Forty-nine machines, from four squadrons, dropped 110 bombs on our aerodrome —or, at least, in its immediate and more remote neighbourhood. The result was poor enough in comparison with the expenditure; our reserve tent was badly perforated and an empty tent—Eschwege's machine was in the air at the time—received some slight slits. An aerial photograph, taken from 200 metres up, showed that even from such a low height it was impossible to ascertain the extent of the damage done. That reconciled us to the affair, because we did not want to allow the Tommies even such a trifling pleasure.

As a rule we limited our own raids to occasional visits by solitary machines. We made some good hits on men and materials, and once we produced a most remarkable psychical effect, as may be seen from the report in H. C. Owen's book :

"I remember one night at a small headquarters mess on the picturesque hills overlooking the Struma valley. The gramophone had been going for some time. And then from out of it a sweet woman's voice sang, 'My ain folk.' Everybody out there had been away from home for two years, and some for over three. The pathos and appeal of the song were almost too much. It hurt. The peace and

beauty of the hills under the moonlight intensified
that sentiment aroused by the gramophone.

"And perhaps it was just as well that just then, up in
the silver blue vault, the hum of a German aeroplane
was heard. In a few minutes it had arrived over the
camp. There was a sudden disquieting whistle of
something coming down and then a flash and a bang,
somewhere close by in the bush that covered the
hills. And again the horrible whistle, and another
flash and a bang. And then the Hun turned his gun
on the camp, which must have looked singularly
pretty. Papapapap! In a few moments he had
passed on. He had not stayed long, but he had
thoroughly conjured away an attack of sentiment,
which, though very charming in amelancholy way,
is not a healthy bedfellow."

CHAPTER VI

EIGHT TO ONE

A MOMENT after landing from a long flight I saw our Bulgarian interpreter running across the aerodrome towards me. I knew something unusual must have happened because Angeloff generally holds fast to the principle of "Poleka! Poleka!"

12. THE ENGLISH AERODROME AT LAHANA : (i) DIRECTION POINTER AND INDICATOR OF NUMBER OF OPPONENTS

13. STAVRO HARBOUR FROM THE AIR

(A gentleman never hurries). He was breathless when he halted in front of me.

" A b—b—big b—b—b—it of n—n—ews ! "

I gathered from his stutter that he was greatly excited by this news, but saw from the gleam in his eyes that it must be good news. I quickly administered a relieving pat on the shoulder. " Tell it slowly ; then we'll get on quicker."

Angeloff made another vain attempt ; then he blurted it out :

" A German submarine ! "

I caught the infection of his excitement. " A German U-boat? That's splendid ! But where ? Has it landed at Kavala ? "

" No ! It's at the station ! "

At first I laughed. But then I reflected that perhaps they had dismantled one, and that it was to be reassembled at Kavala. " So it's only the parts of a submarine ? " I suggested. " But how did you get to know ? "

I felt offended that we, who, after all, might be affected by its arrival, had been left without any official information.

" They're talking about it in the town," he replied.

So the whole business was so secret that even we soldiers were not allowed to know—and yet the whole town knew already. Secrecy was evidently a thing impossible in the Balkans. In any case, it was up to me to probe the matter to the core, and so I mounted my bicycle and rode off to the station.

On the way I thought things over. This reassemblable submarine seemed to be a pure "canard," because our navy would not need to send a U-boat on such a complicated journey. Hersing had taken a submarine from Zeebrugge to Constantinople the previous year

E

by sea ! All the same, there must be something in the rumour, I thought, and felt a strong desire to see at least this gnat which the gossip of the town had inflated into an elephant in the course of a few hours.

And in fact it was only a gnat, although a fairly overgrown one. The reassemblable submarine dwindled down to a motor long-boat belonging to the German Minelaying Department.

. . . . .

At midday we welcomed the officer in command of it as our guest in the mess. He laughed heartily when I told him of the rumours.

"That's always the way with us!" he said. "Whenever people see a small boat and some German sailors, they always turn it into a submarine, but we are only quite harmless mine-layers. You know, gentlemen, that we have to count on the possibility of an Entente landing on Bulgarian soil, and so we're going to take the precaution of laying a few eggs in front of Kavala."

I shook my head. "I don't believe in the idea of a landing."

"To tell you the truth, I don't, either. But no good shutting the stable door after the horse is stolen. In any case, we've booked a small success of sorts. Several days ago an English patrol boat ran on to one of our mines and went ashore."

We shared his joy at it, although, as a matter of fact, we had already received news of the event. We had put it down to trouble with the engines, having no notion that the cause of the mishap was "made in Germany."

. . . . .

Several days later the boat was rocking on the waves of the Aegean, and soon afterwards we were able to pay a visit to our naval comrade in Kavala.

" Well, busy at work ? " we inquired.

The mariner smirked. " Pretty well through, in fact. Just a couple more eggs to put out, and then the job's done ! "

We congratulated him on the speedy accomplishment of his mission. " But haven't the English got wind of you ? " we asked.

" I'm afraid so. Last night the sea was so silent that they must have heard our engine in Thasos. They tried to locate us with their searchlight, but couldn't get a sight of us in this misty weather. Oh, by the way, I remember—we saw a shark on our way back this morning. Take care the brute doesn't get you when you bathe ! "

．　　．　　．　　．　　．

Three days afterwards we received news that the last mines were laid ; altogether a hundred had gone down. Our hearty joy in the fact that our German mariners had not been caught was, however, soon to be clouded, because the close meshes of the net of espionage, which the Entente had woven about us, were bound to catch news of the business sooner or later. They got wind of it all right—but luckily later.

One of their agents contrived to leave the mainland in a small sailing boat and reach Thasos. There he reported the fairy tale of the new submarine with its base at Kavala to the English officer in command, who speedily—but still too tardily—drew his own conclusions.

．　　．　　．　　．　　．

Two days later the thunder of guns roused me from my sleep in the grey dawn. I seized the receiver placed by my bedside and made inquiries.

" English fleet bombarding Kavala," was the news.

So that was their little attention to our sailorman.

" Put me through to Lieutenant Eschwege, please ! —Morning, Eschwege ! Heard the news ? "

" Rather ! Aviation central just told me the ships' guns are directed by ten English planes. I'm off to have a close look at the brethren ! "

I had to laugh. " Well, in that case the bombardment won't last long. Hals und Beinbruch ! "

.   .   .   .   .

I dressed and went out to the aerodrome, where I was just in time to see Eschwege's Albatros climbing up into the pale morning sky. He was not flying towards Kavala, but heading a south-easterly course for the mountains.

Sly fellow ! For naturally the Thasos airmen would keep a sharp look-out in the direction of Drama to prevent Eschwege springing any surprises on them. And so he fetched a compass, which would enable him to come up behind them.

A quarter of an hour later he reached the coast at Vasova Daljani. To his right lay Kavala with its blocks of streets that rose in terraces, its white houses and its verdant gardens, bathed in the red glow of the youthful morning sun. Its crown was the walls of the old Turkish citadel. (Photograph 14.)

But Kavala presented no peaceful picture that day. From the harbour and its adjacent streets the black clouds caused by the explosions of the ships' shells rose up again and again. For out in the roads lay the

English fleet . . . firing. Poor people of Kavaal down below there !

Eschwege flew onward—out to sea. Then he went into a sharp right-hand turn, which gave him the sun at his back, and headed for the English ships. He peered ahead with strained eyes to ascertain the number of machines circling round the fleet. The Bulgarian telephone message had exaggerated it, for he could count only eight instead of ten. Only eight !

A Farman two-seater was flying low. In it sat the artillery observer, who directed the fire of the ships' guns. The other seven—nimble, speedy scouts— were circling round several hundred metres higher. Thus the Farman could note the shell-burst at his ease and wireless down his range corrections. He was guarded by his comrades. Eschwege thought it over quickly. Only one machine came into question, as far as he was concerned—the observation machine. If he could bring it down, the guns on board the English ships would be eyeless, and could gain no further directions for their fire. That would be worth while !

But how to manage it ? The moment he was sighted, the pack of seven would come down on him. So it would have to be a surprise attack ! If it came off—and if the Farman did not sheer away too quickly —and if his guns did not jam—then he could dispose of his victim before the guardian angels arrived on the spot. As he was a thousand metres above them, he could descend on the Farman's neck in a steep nose-dive before the scouts reached him. Moreover, he had the great advantage of flying out of the sun.

A minute later he was ready to go into his nose-dive.

A downward glance ; the English fleet was steaming along in line. Here and there a ray of fire shot out of a barrel, to be followed by a little cloud of smoke, which curled round the sides of the ships. Small, swift craft—the submarine-hunters—circled round the firing warships.

Eschwege peers ahead. Ah, just the right distance —gas switch back a few pegs—machine down on her nose—and dive. Now he is down to the height of the scouts, who continued to fly their circles without troubling about him—now he is below them, hurtling towards the Farman—now he is near enough to it to pull up his stick ever so slightly—now he has the English machine nicely in his sights—but wait a moment—don't shoot yet—not for another ten seconds, until within a hundred metres—only keep a cool head —the burst must go home, and the enemy must go down at the first onslaught—for the seven up there will give him no chance of a second. Never-ending moments of suspense !

As yet the Farman's observer does not seem to be aware of the peril that threatens him. Under the guardianship of his seven comrades, he feels himself as safe as in Abraham's bosom. With his hand on the transmitter, he leans overboard unconcernedly, searching for the shell-bursts.

But now Eschwege is within a hundred metres of him. He has forgotten the seven scouts, for now they cannot save their protégé. He presses the trigger button — tackackackackackack ! The burst goes home, for the lines of the tracer bullets end in the enemy's cockpit.

There—tack-tack-tack-tack-tack—the rattle slows down a bit—the left gun is jammed ! To be hoped the right one will last out !

And it lasts—tacktacktacktacktacktack !

When Eschwege is within twenty metres of the Farman, it goes down by the nose and hurtles seaward. The pilot is hit—he has fallen against the stick. (See sketch at chapter heading.)

Eschwege utilizes the breathing-space to put his machine into a steeply banked right-hand turn, so that he can get a sight of the seven scouts. Meanwhile these latter have recovered from their bad surprise and are swooping down on him from all sides.

A glance below him. The Farman is still falling. A white trail of smoke marks its path. The fuselage with its heavy engine inside drops like a stone into the depths, the light wings flutter after it like falling leaves. . . .

Eschwege draws a deep breath. Victory !

How good to be able to return home with this certain victory ! A quick glance behind him. The seven are following—but the distance between pursuers and pursued has increased somewhat. His machine is now the speedier as he heads for Kavala without worrying about loss of height.

So now he can watch the Farman's engine fall into the sea at his ease. Already the water goes up in spray. Then the sea all round the scene of the crash becomes as smooth as a mirror—a wide circle of oil is spreading out. Slowly the two wings flutter down from the air to the water.

What next ? A fight with the seven scouts ? That would be senseless ! Especially as the left machine-gun has jammed and half the belt of the right one is shot away.

A final backward glance. The scouts have turned back. And down below two submarine-hunters with smoking funnels are churning the water as they hasten to the scene of the crash.

Homeward !

.   .   .   .   .

Meanwhile I waited on the aerodrome in anxious suspense, for no report on the issue of the fight against odds had reached me from the observation posts.

At last the faint drone of an engine comes to me from the direction of Philippi. The ghastly suspense is over. It is his machine, for even though I cannot see it in the morning haze, I know the song of his engine.

Successful or unsuccessful—Eschwege is returning from the fray unharmed. The next moment the telephone in the men's tent almost chirps. I rush inside and obtain the news I want from the aviation central. When Eschwege shot down the English artillery plane, the fleet which was deprived of its eye suspended the bombardment.

As I emerge again on to the aerodrome, Eschwege jumps out of his machine, beaming with joy, and gives me a hug. I quickly inform him of what I have heard. He nods his satisfaction.

" I could see the Farman fall into the sea myself, but it's simply splendid to know that the fleet stopped shooting afterwards."

Meanwhile he has examined his left gun and cleared the jam. " You can imagine what a start it gave me when the gun jammed," he says. " And I can't blame anyone else for the trouble, because I filled the belt myself yesterday ! " Then, turning to his mechanic with a mock threat : " A lucky thing for you. Well, fill the belt up again at once and give the machine some oil and petrol because it's quite possible that the

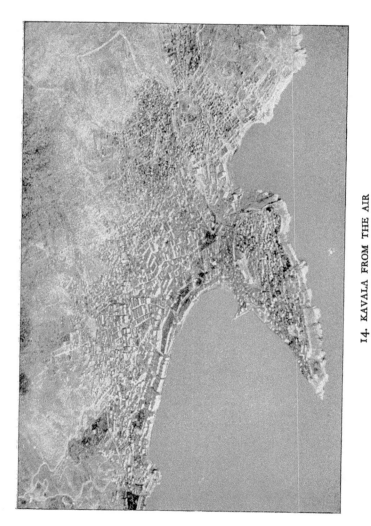

14. KAVALA FROM THE AIR

15. ARCHIE'S VICTIM MAKES A FORCED LANDING AT IRALTI

16. RAILHEAD AT GÜVESNE

17. A DIRECT HIT BY AN ENGLISH BOMB

Thasos brethren will come along for their revenge,
as they will want to make amends for their failure."

I got him into the car with the greatest difficulty.
"Man alive, we'll have a decent breakfast first;
we're starving."

Then he unbuttoned his flying kit with a laugh.
"You're right. But first of all I must wash and dress.
This morning's business was such a quick one that I
really had no time to put on my uniform—I just
buzzed off in my pyjamas."

.   .   .   .   .

We inspected the effects of the bombardment when
we made our next trip to Kavala. Although an
occasional stray shot had wandered into the town, we
had to admit that the guns were brilliantly trained on
the harbour. But what gave us the greatest cause for
wonder was the accurate information of the Entente
agents, for the customs-house, in which the hundred
mines had been stored, was thoroughly smoked out.

But, luckily, the nest was already empty.

.   .   .   .   .

After this fine success we should have been only
too pleased to see a real submarine in Kavala harbour.
But this wish was also fulfilled. An English cruiser
of the Juno class was stationed at Stavro. As far as
we were concerned she was quite harmless, since her
anti-aircraft gunners were vile marksmen. But she
was nevertheless an awkward customer, because she
plastered our line of flight with shellbursts and so put
the English airmen on our track. They found us all
the quicker and were able to hinder our reconnaissances and photography, wherefore we should have
been glad enough to set a German submarine at her.

The chances of this pious aspiration being fulfilled certainly looked slight enough, because the harbour was protected by a mine and net barrage. We could see the huge floats of the nets quite plainly when we flew low over a calm sea, and often had opportunity to do so when returning from flights in that direction, as it was a favourite amusement of ours to assail with our bombs and machine-guns the patrol boat that watched over the net. We were not so greatly influenced by military considerations as by the delicious satisfaction we obtained from creating trouble for the British navy. Moreover, the action of the waves was so pretty when a ship with a smoking funnel tried to dodge our bombs by a course of irregular zigzags.

· · · · ·

But one day the cruiser vanished. We thought she had steamed off on receiving orders to proceed to another station, but soon we learnt something better from the official communiqué.

Despite the shallowness of the water a German submarine forced its way through the barrage into Stavro harbour and sank the old girl with two well-aimed torpedoes.

CHAPTER VII

A RUN OF BAD LUCK

LIEUTENANT LENZ was supposed to be bullet-proof. On nearly every flight he got into some sort of a nasty mess, but he always wriggled out of it and came home without a scratch. As his intangibility became remarkable in the course of time, we gave him the honorary title of " The Virgin."

Whenever he reported himself back from a flight over the lines, he always told his tale in the same matter-of-fact way. It was all the same to him whether he had a hot time or did not see a single tail in the sky.

This virgin appeared to have no nerves at all, and his lack of them pleased me because it was an exception to the general rule.

It is always a pleasure to meet old friends.   Sergeant Stattaus, who piloted me on my first flights on the Western front, had been shot down by French Archies over Châlons.   But he and several comrades succeeded in breaking out of the prison camp at Fort Asnières, near Dijon, and crossing the Swiss frontier at Les Verrières.   After barely seven months of involuntary separation, he was thus able to report to me again, and I allotted him to Lieutenant Lenz for the time being.

.   .   .   .   .

One day Angeloff, our Bulgarian interpreter, announced his presence when we were sitting over our afternoon tea.

" You're wanted at Divisional Headquarters, sir," he told me.

Lieutenant-Colonel Asmanoff received me with a serious face.   " There's something going on in Thasos.   Last night a big transport with an escort of three steamers put in there, and this afternoon three bombing squadrons visited the Sarishaban plain."

I had to agree with him.   There was something queer going on.

" Moreover, as you already know from the communiqué, three warships fired thirty-one shells into Kavala harbour and the neighbouring coast about noon yesterday."

I gave Lenz and Stattaus their orders when I got back.   " I want photos of the aerodrome and the ships lying in the roads.   And you can drop a few eggs on them by way of welcome."

Their Albatros took off at 6.15 p.m. A few minutes later the sun-haze of the hot afternoon swallowed it up somewhere over the mountains round about Philippi.

Divisional H.Q. rang me up about 8 p.m. : " Where are the photos ? " I could only resign myself to report : " Reconnaissance machine not yet back ! "

Tormented by my unrest, I went out to the aerodrome. Again and again I looked at my watch and listened in the direction of Philippi. But I could hear no drone of an engine.

Darkness fell slowly, bringing with it the dread certainty : our comrades are overdue.

. . . . .

What had happened ?

Immediately after taking off Stattaus steered a direct course for the island via Kavala, keeping a sharp eye open for English aircraft. Lenz also bent over and searched the aerodrome ahead with his glasses. There was certainly big business going on over yonder, for six machines stood before the hangars, while in the roads lay a huge transport and three tiny submarine-hunters.

First the photos, then the bombs ! Lenz snaps the ships on to his plates quickly, but when he is just about to turn his camera on to the aerodrome, a most unpleasant surprise makes him put it down again. There are only four machines down below there now, which means that two have taken off. A glance at the altimeter : 3,000 metres. Well, it will take them some little time to climb as high as that. Having instructed Stattaus and taken his photographs of the aerodrome, he replaces the camera in its case.

Then " Crack ! " and once again, " Crack ! " Of course, the Archies are bound to butt in. Moreover, they are taking their job very seriously to-day ; the shell-bursts are most accurate, especially in their elevation. That is doubly unpleasant, since they mark the target for the two scouts.

Lenz bends over quickly and whacks Stattaus into a turn, because he has to fly dead against the wind to drop his bombs. No sign of the two English machines anywhere.

Two more shells. But as the gunners did not foresee the turn, they are not so well placed as the first ones. And now the machine's nose is turned into the wind—the direction is perfect—another three seconds—now then—four times Lenz pushes the lever and then gives a quick glance overboard. Neatly despatched, the four torpedo-shaped bombs whirl earthwards. Bon voyage !

And then—quite near—" Crack ! "

The detonation is so loud that it hurts their ear-drums. The machine gives a jump as though struck by a savage gust. The cloud of smoke from the shell-burst streams out from right underneath them. Something cracks in the engine, and at the same moment another cloud of smoke rises up. A hit ! Stattaus gives an anxious look at the rev-counter, the hand of which drops quickly. Instinctively he throttles down a bit so as to avoid putting too great a strain on the engine and possibly bursting it to pieces. He has done the right thing, for his propeller's revolutions become slower and slower, and finally it comes to a standstill.

A wave of hot blood rises to Stattaus's heart. Will they be able to cross the sea and reach the mainland with their dead engine ? Yes, they can manage it if they may prolong their glide in peace. But the worst is still before them ; they will have to fight their way back against the two scouts, which may loom up any moment. They can only dodge their bursts by going into turns, and every turn means a loss of height and direction. If the two Englishmen keep sitting on them by means of alternating onslaughts and thus prevent them from maintaining a straight glide, a terrible end awaits them, because they will be forced down on to the waves. And as their Albatros is a land machine, with wheels, it will turn turtle badly when put down on the water. Eschwege has demonstrated this often enough at the expense of the Thasos airmen he fought over the sea.

Meanwhile Stattaus heads the machine N.N.E. in order to reach the nearest point of the mainland. A few more shells bursts, but they lie above as well as behind them because the machine has already lost considerable height in its glide.

Lenz takes a look round. The suspense tears at his nerves. If only he could catch sight of the two scouts and so banish the danger of a surprise attack! And there—at last!—barely three hundred metres below them—he sees the gleam of the English cockades.

The two adversaries go into astonished turns when Lenz rattles a few shots down at them. But as they can climb quickly while his own machine continues to glide down, it is not long before they rise above him. And now the first of them attacks, but the well-aimed continuous fire that is his welcome forces him to sheer off quickly. There is no need for Stattaus to go into a turn, and so no height is lost.

The second takes his time over his attack. A few minutes elapse before he dives. He too does not seem to be in a particularly aggressive mood to-day, and so he bears away from the fire he receives. And then the incredible happens; the Englishmen go

gliding back to Thasos.   Probably they did not notice
that our machine's engine is dead ; otherwise they
would have exploited its plight more fully.

.   .   .   .   .

Our men breathed freely.   The worst peril had
mercifully passed them by, for now they did not need
to go into turns.   They had a chance to reach the
mainland in a straight glide.

And so it came to pass.   Slowly the rescuing land
drew nearer.   Now at last they were over the coastal
marshes of Kumburnu and sailing slowly on towards
Iralti.   Well for them that they still had enough
height to cross this evil country and reach dry land.

Deeper and deeper they dropped.   Stattaus gave
an anxious glance down at the ground below, the
uneven patches of which were marked by the sharp
shadows thrown by the setting sun.   Then the
machine landed and taxied for a few metres.   Ah, a
ditch, and running at a slant to their own direction as
well !   Snick !   snack !   the struts of their undercarriage broke away, and at the same moment the
big bird turned turtle.

Lenz and Stattaus scrambled out of their seats.
The unusual attitude of their machine had one advantage ; it enabled them to see the damage done by
the hit without having to bend over.   A shell splinter,
as large as a hand had gone through the crank-box and
smashed a connecting-rod.   (Photograph 15.)

From the nearby Iralti Lenz was able to get in touch
with me by telephone, about ten o'clock.   I passed
his observations on at once to the chief of the staff,
who was very satisfied with them and greatly pleased
to learn that our two airmen had succeeded in reaching
the mainland.   All of us were also glad at this happy
ending—except Eschwege.

" If only I could have known ! " he protested.
" All that time I was pushing round the Struma front,
where there was not a tail to be seen.   And over there
I could have caught two at once ! "

.   .   .   .   .

He sought his consolation the following day, when
Lenz and Stattaus had returned safely to us.   In a
battle of turns he shot a B.E.'s engine to pieces and
forced it to land in the Takhino marsh.   And a few
hours later, the fortunes of war favoured him again,
for the land machine he attacked was forced down on
to the sea with a damaged engine.   (See sketch at
chapter heading.)

A fortnight later an Englishman whom Ahlen had
shot down told us the end of the tragedy.   Both the
officers managed to get clear of the sinking machine
and tried to swim to the nearby island of Thasopulo,
which lies between Thasos and the mainland.   But
only the pilot succeeded ; the observer was drowned.
When night fell, the survivor was rescued by his
comrades, who sent a motor-boat from Thasos for
him.

.   .   .   .   .

At the end of May we received the first indications
that the English were about to take their lines back.
While the camp of canvas in the plain dwindled, the
number of tents on the western slopes of the foothills
increased.

By the middle of July the enemy had completed his
retreat to the right bank, beyond which he only
retained possession of the seven well-developed bridge-
heads at the river crossings.   The reports of our
agents and statements made by prisoners informed
us that this evacuation was due to the cases of malaria

F

and had therefore been ordered for reasons of hygiene. Thus Anopheles Maculipennis, the diminutive malaria fly, succeeded where cannons and machine-guns failed, for he drove the Tommies out of the malaria-infested Struma.

B. J. Seligman, the English war correspondent, has given a vivid description of the situation in his *Macedonian Musings* :

" The plain with its tiny villages, its green shrubbery with here and there a cluster of trees, and the river, twisting its way through like the coils of a giant snake, forms a pleasant and attractive picture. But those who lived last summer by the river banks, stifled with the heat, pestered with insects, stricken with disease, have come to loathe the plain—yes, and fear it as if it were some evil spirit, for they know.

" I remained there only ten days. I shall never forget those ten days as long as I live. Flies and mosquitoes swarm around every camp, yet you have not the strength of will in this living tomb to brush them away from you.

" Last summer we took up our positions by the river banks and clung to them during the summer. God ! How we paid for them in sickness, agony and death. This year we have learnt our lesson ; early in June we abandoned the positions so hardly won and re-crossed the river."

.   .   .   .   .

All the reinforcements and supplies for the English Struma front had to come up the Seres Road from Salonica. In the early days the lorries had to load up in Salonica, but when the main line of railway was pushed up to Güvesne, the motor journey was shortened almost by half.

We had to check the traffic on this important line of communication at frequent intervals, because it was strewn with dumps and depots for supplies of munitions, food and all sorts of materials as well as camps for the troops. The most important points were the camps at Güvesne, Likovan, Lahana, and Gorasanli.

. . . . .

Lieutenant-Colonel Asmanoff discussed the new situation with me in detail.

"According to your photographic reports the railhead at Güvesne is strongly held. (Photograph 16.) Moreover, I have a report from an agent to the effect that the English are planning to build a new field railway alongside of the Seres Road, which is to extend from Likovan *via* Lahana to Gorasanli. If this information is correct, it is for us a valuable confirmation of the fact that we have to deal with a withdrawal for health reasons and not a strategic retreat to the rear positions at Lahana, or even as far back as the Bird Cage fortifications round Salonica. I therefore can give you a very important mission for to-morrow ; it is to ascertain the extent of railway under construction along the road from Salonica to Orljak."

Lenz and Stattaus took off at 5.40 p.m. on this job. I stood on the aerodrome, following their machine with my eyes. In a few minutes the haze swallowed it up.

I was heartily glad at that, for it meant that they would not be sighted so easily when they were across the lines. It was a great advantage for them to-day, because their route took them from Ambelones, near Salonica, where the C Flight of No. 17 Squadron was stationed, along the road to Lahana. There they would find the aerodrome of the B Flight, which contained Captain Green—a person who was not particularly popular in our part of the world.

For a while I still heard the drone of their engine, but the sound grew ever fainter—then it died away, and our last contact with them was broken. . . .

. . . . .

I made work for myself at the aerodrome so that I could be there to receive them when they landed. At about 7.30 p.m. the drone of an engine came to me from the direction of Lake Takhino. The sound came nearer—a German engine ! So once more I could cast off my cares, for five minutes later Lieutenant Lenz was there to give me his report.

" They are really building their field railway, starting at Likovan, but not *via* Lahana. It runs alongside the main road, *via* Hadji Bayramli."

This was the desired confirmation—as welcome to the chief of the staff as to myself. I shook both their hands warmly to show how I rejoiced with them.

" You've done a splendid bit of work ! That was the main thing ! Anything else happened ? "

Lenz pouted.

" Some fierce fights. Naturally, Salonica reported us to Lahana, so that Captain Green caught us over his aerodrome with three machines. I've never been through such a crazy business before. They kept on attacking in turns, so that we did not get a moment's rest. Often enough they caught us in a dangerous burst. We should certainly have been pounded to bits if Stattaus hadn't put us into such splendid turns. They kept their pincers on us a long way behind the lines, right up to Porna station."

I measured the distance off on the map. "That means a running fight of over thirty-four kilometres. Boys, you've had the devil's own luck!" Meanwhile the armoury master had removed the machine-gun and ammunition drums. "The Herr Lieutenant fired 400 rounds," he announced. And while we looked into the cockpit to see the used cartridge cases lying in heaps, the works master examined the machine.

"Eight hits!" was his report.

.   .   .   .   .

One day at the beginning of July I took Lenz aside.

"My dear Virgin Lenz, you have now done enough front patrols for me to put you in for your observer's badge. All you've still got to do is a long distance reconnaissance to Salonica, which you can carry out with Acting-Officer von der Weppen. You can start from Flying Section 30's aerodrome, so that you will have an easier return trip from Salonica. The usual job: photos of aerodromes, camps and shipping."

.   .   .   .   .

Taking off from Hudova, they slipped over the front with a strong north wind at their backs.

Ten kilometres behind the front—and the air still clear. Not a sign of enemy aircraft, not a single shot from an Archie. Lenz searched the sky around him with worried eyes. Where were all the defence forces? But at last the shell for which he had almost been longing burst on his right.

Weppen put the machine instinctively into a left-hand turn. He could not possibly know that in so doing he was placing it straight above another shell, which exploded at that very moment. The mighty detonation almost wrenched the stick from his hand as it banged the machine upward. At the same moment he heard something crack in the engine, which began to rumble. Slower and slower grew the revolutions, until at last they ceased altogether. A hit! A very good hit, in fact! Weppen promptly put the machine's nose round and headed for the lines.

Lenz leans over to him anxiously. "Can we get back to Hudova in a glide?"

He has no need to shout to make himself understood, for the engine is dead. Weppen shrugs his shoulders and glances at the altimeter. Four thousand metres.

"Perhaps—if we're lucky!"

They have no luck. The sharp north wind which made the outward trip child's play, offers a hard resistance to them on the return journey and brakes their speed considerably. Slowly, ever so slowly, Lake Doiran creeps towards them, and quickly, far too quickly, the slender hand of the altimeter goes back. 3,500 metres . . . 3,000 . . .2,500 . . .2,000 . . . 1,500 . . . they can only hope that at least they will get over the Bulgarian lines!

Now they are once more within range of the Archies of the front. Under no circumstances would it be pleasant to be peppered by them at such a low height, but to-day it is the very devil. For their bird cannot make any long turns to get out of range; they eat up too much of the precious height. Yet rather thirteen Archies than one enemy scout! If a scout attacks them fiercely, they must worm their way out of his bursts; if they have to do that several times, they will never cross the lines.

Lenz looks round anxiously. But this time, at least, luck seems to be with them. The sky is void of aircraft

Doiran and its lake lie on their left. Slowly the English trenches approach them. And then a witches' Sabbath breaks loose ; every field battery cherishes the ambition of bringing the German machine down before it flies over the lines. A lucky thing for them that the gunners have no experience in dealing with aerial targets and so set their fuses incorrectly.

But a large pack is bound to kill the hare. Now the rifles and machine-guns of the trenches also join in. Their rattling and barking seem to mount up from every quarter of the heavens. They can hear the noise plainly through the song of their bracing wires. The worried Weppen goes into irregular zigzags. How long can they go on before one of these fearsome steel and leaden scythes catches them and cuts them in pieces. . . .

Now they have only 500 metres of height left. Lenz can endure the inactive suspense no longer. He pulls the butt end of his machine-gun against his cheek and rakes the trenches. At least his bullets will make the Tommies aim nervously or send them to cover. As soon as one ammunition drum is finished, he puts another in. But just as he is about to re-open fire, he drops the butt in glad surprise and bends over to Weppen.

" We've passed the English front lines ! "

Weppen gives him a nod of pleasure and then peers ahead anxiously. They are barely 200 metres up and cannot reach the Bulgarian positions, which are a long distance away from the English ones. They will have to land somewhere between the lines.

Deeper and deeper they drop—now the wheels touch the ground—a little hop—and then their bird taxies cleanly onward. But the fire of the English batteries starts before it comes to a standstill.

Luckily, the first shells burst a good distance away, so that Lenz has time to photograph the damage. A shell splinter has pierced the crank-box from below and smashed a connecting rod—just as it did three weeks ago when he flew to Thasos with Stattaus !

Coincidence !   Coincidence ?

Lenz gathers up his camera and plates while Weppen dismounts the pivotable machine-gun.   Then it is high time for them to decamp, for the shells are bursting appreciably nearer.   They scurry northward at a run towards the Bulgarian trenches which beckon them.   At the village of Akindshali they meet the first sentinels, from whom they receive a friendly welcome.

.   .   .   .   .

After getting on the telephone to me, Lenz waited at Akindshali with Wappen until nightfall, because they wanted to salve what was left of the machine. The English batteries fired four hundred shells at it, and a flight of eight machines bombed it, but when twilight set in, our couple went back to it with a Bulgarian patrol. Although the English artillery was still engaged on its work of destruction, they succeeded in salving the engine and the rigid machine-gun.

CHAPTER VIII

OUR FRIENDS THE TURKS

OUR friends the Turks.

The Turks were always good comrades to us, as long as we were on the ground with them. As soon as we flew, there was an end to the friendship. Faithful to their adage " Ak köpek kara köpek, ikisside köpek dir " (White dog or black dog, both are dogs), they fired on every aeroplane, irrespective of whether it bore a cross or a cockade, so that we had to suffer equally with the English from their pleasure in shooting. My requests, complaints and protests were all received with a kindly smile.

" Af ederssinis ! " (We beg your pardon.)

They promised to give strict instructions and punish the culprits severely ; they almost went as far as to promise to send the severed heads of the delinquents to my house. Nevertheless everything went on as before, and we therefore sought consolation in trying to see the humour of the situation.

One evening we had a jüzbaschi (Turkish captain) as a guest in our mess and discussed with him this false conception of the term " blood-brotherhood." He shrugged his sholuders.

" Pek me jussum ! " (I'm very sorry.)

I continued, with a wink to my companions :

" We've been trying to find the reason and we have hit on three of them. We would like you to tell us which is the right one. Ischit (listen.)

" Reason 1 : The recognition mark of our aeroplanes is a cross. Your people have still got the old challenge in their blood : ' the crescent must conquer the cross ! ' It is therefore no wonder that your guns almost go off of their own accord on religious grounds.

" Reason 2 : With the exception of those drawn from the towns, your soldiers are enemies of everything that is modern. A man who flies is a son of Sheitan, the devil. Sheitan must be destroyed.

" Reason 3 : By an oversight His Majesty the Sultan signed an old decree relating to former wars, which ends with the words: ' Olüm, hep gjaur! ' (Death to all the infidel Christian dogs.) So what can your soldiers do but obey it ? "

The jüzbaschi laughed.

" None of these three reasons is correct. Listen to the fourth and right one. Our people always think the English might have painted crosses instead of cockades on their wings as a ruse of war. Naturally I know, as well as you do, that this is extremely improbable. But our asskerlar (soldiers) have got the belief firmly fixed in their heads. If we could make it clear to them that the cross-bearing aeroplanes are not disguised English machines, then, of course, they would not fire at them, for, as you have experienced when you met us, gentlemen, it is not only we officers who love the alamandscha tajaradschilar (German airmen); every soldier loves them too. We call them bisim tajaradschilar (our airmen), and so hejdi bisim tajaradschilar alamandscha! (long live our German airmen!)"

We thanked him heartily, for he had really made a very nice excuse to clear himself and his people. But, nevertheless, we decided to hold fast for the future to the wise advice: "Eschejini ewel bagla ssonra tanryja issmarla!" (God watches over your donkey, but tie him up as well), and so flew over the Turkish sector at such a great height that their tokens of erring love could not reach us.

. . . . .

Several months later one of the Turkish divisions in our sector and the H.Q. of the 20th Turkish Army Corps were transferred elsewhere. When the 50th Division followed them after a brief space, its commander expressed his thanks for the support we had given him in a most laudatory order of the day. I handed Eschwege a translation of this.

"Really, we ought to thank Shükri for his kind words," I suggested. "We might take off to-night and chuck him down a fat bouquet of flowers when he's entraining with his staff."

Eschwege laughed wryly. "And what'll you

report to the Kofl[1] if I crash a machine on landing in the pitch darkness ? "

I screwed up my left eye. " In the first place you won't crash because you can see in the dark like an owl. Secondly it's not dark at all, because the moon's nearly full. And thirdly, we can whitewash the business by hooking it on to a spot of raiding on Thasos."

And so it came to pass.

Having packed a couple of hundredweights of bombs into our machine, we flew several turns round the railway station at a low height—firing a lot of starshells in order to prevent the Turks from answering our friendly farewell greeting with unfriendly volleys. The bouquet we dropped down landed most correctly on the railway lines. I let Eschwege cut his engine and we shouted in chorus our carefully-rehearsed " Allaha issmarladyk ! " (May Allah preserve you !) three times from a height of 200 metres.

Then we headed for Thasos.

.   .   .   .   .

It is a splendid moonlit night which would have rejoiced the heart of the poet Eichendorff.

The Kavala road shimmers like a dull silver-grey ribbon. When we have flown over the ruins of Philippi, we see the foothills bordering the farther side of the lake all a-glitter. Ten minutes later we have left the coast behind us. The sea's surface is only little curly waves, on which the moonlight breaks up into a thousand facets.

To Thasos !

But meanwhile the folk on the island have grown lively. A searchlight flashes up and gropes for us

---

[1] Kofl = Kommandeur der Flieger (Officer in command of the Air Service).

through the milk-white air with its quivering ray. Then it goes out again.

Our craft drones its way through the moonlight in a steady flight. Again the searchlight flashes up. It explores the sky nervously, but can find nothing. Once it touches our machine, but overlooks us and goes wandering on like a will o' the wisp. I am feeling satisfied; it is not one of those powerful ship's searchlights; the illumination it gives is so feeble that it does not dazzle us, but even provides a good line of direction.

And now the soft outlines of the island's blue mountains take clear shape in the moonlight. We shall reach our objective in a few minutes. The searchlight becomes very nervous; up and down, hither and thither it flashes.

Then the defence forces begin to get to work even before we have reached the coasts of the island. The quickfirer sends up her phosphorus shells, which rise at regular distances from each other, looking like gleaming strokes—from ten to twenty golden rods, one behind the other.

But to-day, as on other occasions, the quickfirer is shooting in a wrong direction. I smile as I think of the yarn I invented about it, namely that the gun-layer of the "stuttering gun" is married to a German girl, who has strictly forbidden him to fire on her fellow-countrymen. But the Tommies also refuse to take their "stuttering gun" seriously, for they have given her the nickname of "Coughing Clara."

The searchlight has better luck to-day. It catches our machine in its beam and tries to keep hold of it. I rattle an accurate continuous fire down at it, which causes its extinction. Its crew must have fled to cover.

Then the quickfirer also becomes silent, so that I can whack Eschwege on to the row of large hangars at my ease.

He flies a perfect course to the mark, so that I can drop all my bombs straight away. Some expectant moments—and then—one !—two !—three !—four !—five !—six !—seven !—eight ! flash up the hits down below there. They lie nice and close to the hangars, even if the desired direct hit has not materialized.

Home again !

Half an hour later we make a good landing on our aerodrome.

.   .   .   .   .

The next morning I asked Captain von Bardeleben, who had hitherto held the post of liaison officer to the Turks, how the divisional commander had liked our ovation. Bardeleben laughed somewhat sourly.

" Oh, he was very pleased at your little attention, and especially with the beautiful bouquet with the ribbons of German and Turkish colours. The only trouble was that we felt a bit worried about the possibility of your making a mistake and handing out a bomb instead of the flowers. And so we didn't really appreciate your act of homage properly until after you had buzzed off."

We laughed heartily. A mistake of that sort would certainly have been a painful one.

.   .   .   .   .

I had been having a talk with Lieutenant-Colonel Asmanoff and was about to take my leave.

" Wait a moment, there's something else," he said. " We've got a second report from our agents to the effect that the English employed spies to set your canvas hangars on fire."

I smiled somewhat incredulously, because I considered these reports to be pure fiction. But I should have been somewhat more thoughtful, I must admit, if I had known the real extent of the 16th Wing's activities, for it has since been narrated that Lieutenant W. S. Scott, of No. 17 Squadron, was able to land an agent in the Drama plain on December 17th, 1916, and another on January 1st, 1917. So it would appear that these two gentlemen paid us an incognito visit at the time mentioned.

Nevertheless the misgivings expressed by Lieutenant-Colonel Asmanoff left me uneasy. I therefore called the Staffel together that same afternoon and put them wise.

" If anyone of you goes under in an airfight, that is destiny. But if a spy burns the roof over our heads, it's our own fault. So keep your eyes skinned ! "

.   .   .   .   .

Soon afterwards my uneasiness received fresh nourishment. A two-seater pilot put a spy down on a patch of waste land, but could not take off again, because he cracked off a wheel on landing. The machine was captured by the Bulgarians ; the pilot managed to disappear, but the agent was taken and executed the following day, with due ministrations of the Church.

After this incident I considered it inadvisable to entrust the safety of the aerodrome's extensive buildings to the guardianship of one solitary picket. As I could not exact further night duty from my Staffel after their strenuous exertions of the day's work, I applied for assistance to Lieutenant-Colonel Münir, the officer in command of the Turkish recruit depot, which still remained in Drama.

" Bujuk memnunijet ile, ssewgülü kardash ! " (It will be a thousand pleasures for me, dear brother !) he replied. In his good comradeship he put so many men at my disposal that none of my own people needed to mount guard thenceforth. (See sketch at chapter heading.)

The Turkish soldiers kept a good watch on our aerodrome, and no act of incendiarism took place.

.   .   .   .   .

I arranged to have a bomb-proof shelter dug near each hangar for the protection of the mechanics in cases of raids. As we could not delve too deep into the soil on account of subterranean water, we had to content ourselves with shallow trenches, roofed over with boards, upon which stones were piled up. We used up all the little wood at our disposal for this purpose, so that we had no materials left over for building huts. It was impossible to procure further supplies from the countryside, which was so deficient in forests, and consequently we were dependent on materials reaching us by rail. Their transport always took a long time ; as the direct railway line was cut by the front, the supplies from our base depot at Nish had to go round by Sofia, Adrianople, Ferejik and Xanthi. This was a stretch of 850 kilometres, or the equivalent of the distance between Berlin and Paris, whereas the actual distance, as the crow flies, was only 300 kilometres—the distance between Berlin and Cassel.

To add to our troubles, the railway from Adrianople onward consisted of a single track only. If we sent one of our men to accompany the stuff and he made a row, and the consignment was then shunted on to a siding " till further notice," it took at least a week to reach us. But if the consignment travelled

18. THE SEAPLANE STATION AT XANTHI

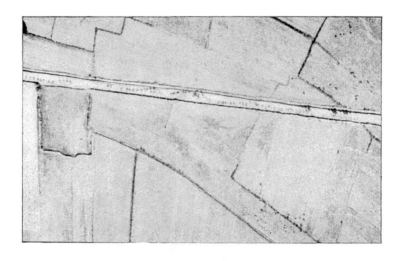

19. CAVALRY ON THE MARCH

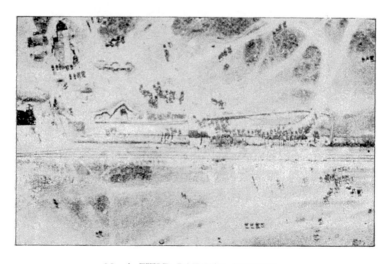

20. A FIELD RAILWAY STATION

unescorted, we had to count on six to eight weeks passing before we got it. Tschakete malko ! (Just be patient for a moment !)

As we were thus without materials for permanent buildings for members of the technical personnel who had to be on the spot always, we housed them temporarily in a canvas hangar.

. . . . .

One night a loud detonation rouses me from my sleep about 3 a.m. An English bomb raid ? And then I hear the drone of an engine. By the sound of it that Tommy cannot be more than 300 metres up.

A red glow pervades my room before the next bomb goes off. My hands stands still when I rush out on to the veranda in dismay. A direct hit on the northernmost tent ! On the tent where we keep the reserve one-seater, on the tent where my seven fellows sleep ! It is blazing up to heaven in a mighty flame !

And my lads, my lads ! I snatch up the telephone receiver and turn the handle. No answer ; the bomb has cut the connection !

Only to know—to know for certain ! An overcoat over my sleeping suit—my feet into their boots—and then out I run to the aerodrome ! Five further bombs go off. The tent is one huge torch.

Now the Very lights are going up. Red and green balls of fire shoot out from the sea of flames and career in long curves. Some signal cartridges follow them, exploding in the air with faint cracks and pouring a shower of white stars on the aerodrome. Then the machine-gun ammunition begins to explode.

" Knack—knackackack—knackack—knackackack-ack—knack ! It sounded just like our protection fire in 1914.

I am out of breath, but I rush on. My men, my men! The airman circles round the aerodrome again and drops another bomb. The livid flash when it comes in contact with the ground gleams on his cockades. You dog, if only I could bring you down!

And then the drone of the engine grows fainter. The Englishman is flying back to Thasos.

As I run on, I hear someone call my name. Eschwege! He has not even got his boots on—only house shoes. When we reach the tent at last, we have to duck because the bullets from the exploding munitions buzz round our ears. At the sound of my voice figures emerge from the night into the glare of the blaze. Leonhardt is the first one whom I can identify.

" Anyone wounded ? "

" No, sir ! "

I am deeply moved by these joyful tidings and can hardly believe my luck. The transition from black grief to bright joy is too sudden. Come here, all seven of you! I must hear your voices, I must see with my own eyes that all the bones in your bodies are unbroken! Full of happiness, I grasp each man's hand—the hands of Brammertz, the armoury master and the six mechanics—Leonhardt and Sichter, Osterwald and Kurtenbach, Szymanski and Freytag. And only then can I breathe freely again from the depths of a joyful heart. It is really true—all seven have been preserved to me!

" Boys, you don't know how glad I am that you managed to get out in time. And no one reported the raider ? "

They were able to laugh again. " No, the sly fellow didn't fly the direct way, but went round by the mountains. And so the observation post didn't hear him ! "

" And you didn't wake up till you heard the bomb?"

Leonhardt's face was thoughtful. " It would have been too late then. The first bomb made a direct hit on our tent, and it was a heavy one."

A shiver ran through my limbs once more. " And nevertheless nothing touched you ? "

" It would have been all up with us if our Turk hadn't kept a sharp look-out. He heard the airman coming and woke us up. We bolted for the dug-out at once, and it was high time, too ! The last of us was still on the steps when it came down, and the air pressure of the direct hit blew him right down on to us ! "

Then they promptly set about the work of extinguishing the blaze. They raked the burning tent to pieces with iron bars and actually succeeded in salving a few things. Leonhardt sustained several burns from glowing scraps of canvas, but luckily, his injuries were not serious.

We then attacked the fire with entrenching tools. But meanwhile we shook our Turk's hand.

" Eji arkadash ! " (Good comrade !)

I am ashamed to say that I can no longer recollect the name of this stout fellow. Allah mukafatinizi werssin, bilmem türk assker ! (May Allah requite thee, thou unknown Turkish soldier !)

.   .   .

Soon afterwards other officers and men came along. The Englishman had really had a great stroke of luck. A direct hit on the tent ! The petrol that spurted out would have sufficed to set the whole tent on fire in the space of a few seconds. (Photograph 17.) We found the charred corpses of our two dogs when we cleared

up the mess. Poor fellows ! In the hurry of the
retreat no one thought of waking them. And I was
still full of gratitude for the wonderful preservation
of my brave fellows. Then suddenly an idea occurred
to me.

"I'd like to bet the Thasos brethren will come
along in the morning for a picture of the damage.
A whole squadron of them naturally, because of
Eschwege. But I think we're going to spoil their
fun for them ! "

I turned to the works master. "Get a lorry and
fetch the reserve tent out of store at once ! We'll
put it up over the scene of the fire and so diddle the
English about the success of their raid."

No sooner said than done. An hour later we had
collected all the debris from a wide area, and over the
blackened ground of the conflagration rose up a new
tent.

.   .   .   .   .

We awaited the morning visitor with much excitement. And—to our great glee—he came ! The
telephone started to ring just before 11 a.m.

"Flight of five machines took off from Thasos ! "

Half an hour later the observation machine, which
was to do the photography, appeared at a respectful
height, accompanied by two one-seaters. Two other
scouts circled in the air above Philippi, waiting to
join the trio on their return.

Our laughter chimed across the aerodrome. Firstly,
it tickled our vanity most agreeably to know that the
enemy respected our prowess to the extent of taking
such precautions. And secondly we pictured the
faces of the Tommies when they developed their
plates and found the usual complete set of tents on

them. The bomb-dropper would have certainly put in an enthusiastic report on his—undoubtedly excellent—results, but by his own estimate of his feat he would henceforth be regarded as an incorrigible optimist. Joy at the misfortunes of others is the purest form of joy.

CHAPTER IX

THE FIRE-RAISERS

MY Staffel was the only German fighting unit in the sector of the 2nd Bulgarian army. The German seaplane station at Xanthi, on Lake Buru, which lay about eighty kilometres eastward of us,

came within the sphere of the Bulgarian 4th army.
(See photograph 18.) It took its orders from the
naval authorities and its main work consisted of
over-sea reconnaissances.

Our naval comrades suffered severely from malaria
in the marshy coastal lands. It therefore came to
pass that Lieutenant Immisch, of the Imperial Navy,
was the only officer in Xanthi. When he met with
a fatal accident while bathing, I had to despatch
Lieutenant Greiff to take command of the station and
undertake the reconnaissance and defence work in
that locality.

. . . . .

The Greek summer brought with it a paralysing
heat. The mercury in the thermometer rose to over
50; then it climbed to 60 and wandered slowly up
towards the 70 mark. The roads and streets were
deserted in the midday hours. Anyone who was
rash enough to leave his house at this time found the
sun beating down upon him so unmercifully that
within half an hour he made an anguished retreat for
the protective shade, where he cursed his folly.

Our bathing place at Kavala lost its popularity;
the warm sea-water affected the skin like an unpleasant
alkali. The cold springs of the town pond, however,
still afforded some refreshment.

We had to carry out our flights in the early morning
and late afternoon, and even then we often flew in our
shirt sleeves. Photography was inconceivable in the
midday heat, because the gelatine layers on the plates
came loose from the glass and threw up blisters.
In the dark-room we had to keep our developer and
fixing-bath on ice.

But under these circumstances we made a virtue

of necessity. The long shadows on photographs taken when the sun was so low in the sky made them extremely plastic—as may be seen in most striking fashion on the two photographs of Flying Section 34 and the Vardar Sector. (Photographs 19 and 20.)

Moreover, our engines proved to be unreliable in the heat of the sun. The heavy oil became as liquid as water; it squirted about in the crank-box and oozed from all joints. It dirtied the bright canvas of the cockpit, drenched one's clothing and coated the goggles. The engine beat as irregularly as a sick man's pulse and put fear into the airmen's hearts, for it is a bad business to fly over the enemy's country or the rugged mountains of the wild Balkan ranges with a knocking engine. Once Lieutenant Rottka and Acting Officer von der Weppen had to break off their front patrol because the hot oil fouled their engine to such an extent that it dropped a full 200 revs.

Thus there seemed to be a tacit agreement between us and the enemy that there was to be no flying in the middle of the day! This lasted until the English made Eschwege an unspoken reason for breaking the agreement. As the principal business was concentrated into a few hours, he was able to achieve greater successes in his flying time.

.   .   .   .   .

We sat at our evening meal—the usual bread and dripping, with tomatoes. Windows and doors were wide open, but the gauze screens in front of them protected us from the mosquitoes. Then my orderly announced Lieutenant Kerikoff.

" The fire raisers are at work again, sir ! "

The news gave me quite a big shock at first, for I was always worried about the possibility of some spy putting a light to our aerodrome.

" Have you caught one ? " I asked.

He smiled. " No, you can do that. You see, they are the English naval airmen from Thasos, and they're having another shot at setting fire to our wheatfields in the Sarishaban plain ! Please help us ! "

" Do the Englishmen land for the job ? "

" Oh no, they daren't do that. But they've fixed up a special kind of incendiary bomb. We made our men collect the fragments, and I can show you them now."

He bade two Voyniks (soldiers) drag in a mighty sack and empty its contents on the floor.

" Tuk ! (here !) They are huge metal pear-shaped containers, filled with petroleum and benzine. When they come down, the impact splits their thin walls, and the squirting liquid is set on fire by an igniter. The next moment you have a circle of about ten metres diameter in flames."

" And do you think the English have any success with these bombs ? "

" Yes. At least they did us a lot of damage with them last year. Certainly the conditions were particularly favourable for them, because the summer was abnormally dry, even for Macedonia. Meanwhile we have collected experiences and organized fire-fighting squads among our men and the villagers. We beat the fire down with sticks and then extinguish it by pouring on earth. We also check it by digging wide trenches in the direction of the wind."

" But isn't the harvesting going on now ? "

" Yes, but all the same, there's a big risk. Our peasants don't cut their corn with scythes, but just take off the ears with their sickles. So the stalks remain standing and give fuel to the fire."

I nodded to Eschwege. " Well, then, off you go,

old man. You've got a forward landing ground at Iralti. Perhaps you can do something."

Eschwege turned to Kerikoff. "About what time do the fire-raisers generally come over?"

"Mostly between 11 a.m. and 3 p.m. Never in the early morning, because the dew is still lying, and very seldom in the late afternoon, because you are about! They came about half-past eleven this morning."

"All right. I'll be on the spot!"

.   .   .   .   .

The following morning Eschwege lay in the thin grass at Iralti.

The sun rose in the sky, but there was no sign of the enemy. He went to his machine and consulted the chronometer. It was close on eleven. The Thasos folk were due soon if they meant to carry out their programme on the lines of the previous day.

He gazed longingly to southward, where the dark blue mountains of Thasos—barely twenty-five kilometres away—towered up to the metallic sky in jagged pinnacles. On the level coastal strip at their feet the Thasos squadron, with its twenty machines or more, had its aerodrome, in the neighbourhood of Megalo Kavamiti. He had already brought down five of them and hoped the sixth would fall that day.

The sun stabbed him. He gave another look to the ammunition belts in the two machine-guns and then lay down in the shadow of the left wing. Wait, wait, wait—that was his only solution of the problem. And how sad it would be to have to fly back home without having seen a single tail.

At last—the drone of an engine! Eschwege jumps up and turns his glasses in the direction of the island. Nothing to be seen! But it is quite likely that the haze is masking the aircraft. He puts his glasses down again and listens eagerly. Yes, again there is that delicious music!

On with jacket and helmet! The drone comes nearer; by the sound of it there must be several machines. But still nothing in sight. Up with the glasses! Ah, yonder over Cape Kojun Nakla three black smears are looming out of the haze.

But patience! No good charging them blindly; the first thing is to find out whether they are flying here or towards some other objective. A nerve-wracking delay of several minutes, during which the glasses remain glued to his eyes.

They are coming this way! They are the fire-raisers! With two leaps Eschwege is at his propeller, swinging it to set the engine going at once. Then he puts his glasses to his eyes again. Now he can recognize them quite plainly. They are flying very low; only about a thousand or twelve hundred metres, he judges. He trembles with joy! They are coming! they are coming!

He thinks it over quickly. He will let them drop their bombs and then catch them by surprise on the way home. Nearer and nearer they come. . . .

Now he can make them out with the naked eye. Two big Farmans with the bombs, and a Sopwith seaplane for their escort. He can see the floats below the wings quite plainly. Just a few minutes more, and then I'll nab you. He would prefer to fly to meet them, but then they would see his approach, and the basis of his anticipated success—the surprise attack—would go to the devil.

So best to wait, however hard it may be. They will not spot his machine so easily as long as it remains down here, for the fuselage and the upper wing surface are painted a dull colour which tones in with the barren land when viewed from above.

Now they are flying over him. Eschwege has to look straight up at them. The observer in one of the Farmans bends over, peering ahead ; he must be looking for his objective. And now they have passed over him ; the mighty harmony of their three engines is dying away. And now two—three—four objects detach themselves from the bulk of the machine. Bombs !

Eschwege feels himself electrified. Those bombs must come down hardly a thousand metres away from him. He climbs into his machine and stands up on the seat to get a better view of the hits.

" Humm ! " the first one ! No detonation and only very little dust. A dud ! Eschwege laughs aloud in malicious glee. But the other three bombs explode : " Crack ! crack !! crack ! ! ! "

A jet of flame hisses out of the dust round the spot where it fell, and then a snow-white pillar of smoke towers up like a slender tree-trunk. A few seconds later its summit begins to spread.

Three such silver pine trees have grown out of the earth. At the same moment the corn around their feet begins to glow and smoulder. Now the other Farman discharges its load of bombs and conjures more magic trees from the parched earth. Then the machines go round in a prolonged turn to head southward. (See sketch at chapter head.)

Now's the time ! Quick as lightning, Eschwege slips into his seat and turns the starter. But the sparking plugs will not work. Another frantic turn of the starter. Again no ignition ! Damn !

Barely a thousand metres above his head, the three machines are on their way back to Thasos, and the drone of their engines sounds like a paean of triumph. No, that must not be! They must not escape! That would be terrible!

In the twinkling of an eye he is out of his machine, swinging the propeller once more. Then back into his seat and round with the starter. But the propeller stands there as stiff as a post and refuses to move. Enough to drive anyone mad! The three machines drone on incessantly towards their home aerodrome. Once again he jumps out and swings the propeller— but for the third time no ignition follows!

Out with the oil-can—open the cocks—some petrol in the cylinders—shut cocks—swing prop again! Now comes the moment which will decide whether he can catch the fire-raisers. He can hardly make them out now with the naked eye ; the haze will have swallowed them. Back again into his seat with his heart thumping out its fear—round with the starter —and—hurrah—the spark catches—the propeller is turning! Heavenly music!

In an instant he has the straps round his shoulders and fastened. Down with the goggles—open throttle gradually—now the engine is giving her full revs— the whirling propeller looks like a glass circle—the machine begins to move slowly—it gets up speed as it taxies—several hops over ridges in the ground— pull stick—in the air—a look ahead! No sign of those three machines now, but I'll catch you all the same!

A minute later his eye picks them out of the haze once more. And now his swift machine comes nearer and nearer to the trio. Can he catch up in time?

Can he? He must!

And even if he has to engage them over their own aerodrome, one at least must fall! The engine only just caught on in time, for now he is already over the huts of Daljan, which lie close to the coast. But he is within 500 metres of them and has climbed 300 above them.

The three are quite carefree. Their job is done. The scout that acts as escort seems to be in the greatest hurry of all to get home again, for he is at least a thousand metres ahead of the slower bombers.

That is all to the good. Yes, now he is just at the right distance for a dive on the hindermost Farman. The observer has not seen him yet. Perched on his tip-up seat, he is reading.

Eschwege puts his machine down on to her nose and bridges the gap in his quick dive.

The observer still has his back turned to him. Yes, now—another hundred metres—the machine is nicely in his sights—press trigger button—and " tackack-ack ! " rattles the burst into the English machine.

Eschwege sees the observer jump up in dismay and pull his machine-gun round. Too late, my friend ! If I've got my burst on you at this distance, then—ah, the gun's jammed ! He has barely space to pull his machine up to avoid ramming the English-man and pass out just above him.

A bad business. But for the gun jam the Tommy would be whizzing down seaward now. Eschwege swears. What does it help him if he can clear the gun again in a few seconds ! His winning trump—the surprise attack—has slipped from his hand.

And now he has to tackle a second opponent as well. While the other Farman puts its nose down and dives for Thasos, the Sopwith scout has turned round immediately at the sound of the firing and is attacking Eschwege from a distance of 300 metres. After emitting a short series of bullets, he turns away again.

Eschwege looks round. What has happened to his Farman? Nowhere to be seen? Has he finished it off with a couple of shots? That would be really wonderful!

But, unfortunately, that is not the case, for now he sights it far below, making for the nearby coast. After him! Never mind if the Sopwith tries to fasten on to his tail again—the main thing now is to get up the right speed by an energetic dive, so that the enemy scout cannot catch him up before he shoots.

So down with the machine on to her nose and after the Farman we go. High time, if we're to catch him, for the coast of Thasos looms alarmingly near. The enemy must not reach it!

Ah, now he is within range again. Through the roar of his engine he hears the two guns of the English observer rattling away. But they shall not spoil his aim. Only don't shoot too soon! Get close up first!

Now! Press trigger button—and now his twin bursts hail into the English machine. The observer goes on shooting—then a cloud of smoke rises suddenly from the engine—the propeller goes slower —and finally Eschwege sees it drop dead. The engine is shot to pieces, and now the Farman will have to go down into the sea. It cannot reach the safety of the shore.

Shall he put another burst in? No; quite un-necessary, for now the observer relinquishes his machine-gun and switches on the dual control device by his seat. The pilot is disabled. The English machine goes down to the waves in a slow glide. As it is a land machine, with wheels, Eschwege knows that it must smash up when it touches the water's surface.

So now he can look round for the Sopwith again. But its pilot seems to have made the same observations and drawn the same conclusions. In any case, he has turned away and is making for his moorings ; he has gone to seek help for his comrades who will be drifting on the sea in a few seconds.

Thus Eschwege can watch the last act of the tragedy at his ease. The observer tries to pull his machine up again when it is close to the water's edge, but the momentum of his glide is exhausted—the wheels touch the water and at the same moment the suddenly braked machine turns turtle. The tail breaks off.

Only 500 metres to the shore. So the two will be able to save themselves by means of their swimming-vests. And the victor is glad of that. The machine is finished completely. Wings and tail are still floating on the waves ; the fuselage has gone down to the depths with the heavy engine.

Eschwege can plainly see the airmen grasping the wreckage and pulling off their yellow leather coats. So the pilot is not dead, but only wounded.

He returns their greeting when they wave up to him. " No, I'm not going to fire at you, poor fellows ! "

Then he heads his machine homeward again.

.   .   .   .   .

Divisional headquarters passed us on the report of the observation post on the coast as we sat over our afternoon tea. Immediately after the two surviving machines landed, a large seaplane took off and cruised over the scene of the wreck for about an hour, in company with a small motor boat. No one could see whether their efforts were successful.

21. ESCHWEGE'S ALBATROS

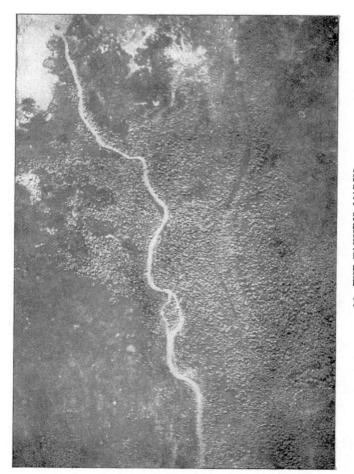

22. THE TAKHINO MARSH

" My Farman is finished," Eschwege opined.   " I hope they were able to fish out the crew."

.   .   .   .   .

Several weeks later Eschwege shot down another Thasos machine over the mainland.   As both pilot and observer fell into our hands unwounded, we were able to inquire after the fate of the their two comrades who had come down in the sea.

" The observer was rescued.   The pilot, who was badly wounded, sank and was drowned."

Eschwege's face grew sad.

" I'm sorry ! " he said.

H

CHAPTER X

3 = o

I

ESCHWEGE strolled about the aerodrome, waiting for news of something in the air. At last good tidings came to hand.

" English machine making for Porna ! "

So jump in and take off ! Infinite minutes of suspense, for each of them brings him only three kilometres nearer the desired goal. He hopes he can locate the Englishman in the strong haze. But there —thank you, dear Archies—the dainty snowballs of shell-bursts take shape in the sky.

Meanwhile the B.E.—a one-seater—has unloaded his cargo of bombs and is making for the lines again. As he has no observer to guard his back, Eschwege can close up with him unseen. But he does not over-climb him for fear the pilot should catch sight of him in his mirror. He prefers to keep under his tail. (Photograph 21.)

He is going to try a new method to-day. As soon as he is close enough, he will put his stick down hard and utilize the speed thus obtained to zoom up sharply and put his burst into the disagreeably sur-prised Tommy from below. He does so, and only after a few seconds has the assailed Englishman recovered sufficiently to throw his machine round and give battle. For a brief space they interchange shots.

But when the Englishman has noticed that Esch-wege is the quicker on his turns and can therefore sit on him again and again after a short pause, he tries to escape over Lake Takhino by a steep dive. Eschwege, however, refuses to let go, and repeatedly forces him to turn at bay. The enemy must go down, because he is shooting at close range, and his burst often gets home.

But unfortunately he does not go down. The two adversaries are only twenty metres above the ground when they reach the marshy land on the farther side of the lake. Now it is high time to finish the business, thinks Eschwege, and sends him a blessing from both guns at once, delivering it from behind at close range.

Ah—left gun jammed! If only the right one can carry on. But that likewise begins to stutter and finally goes on strike. Full of rage, Eschwege bends over and clears both guns. Then he goes into a turn in order to give the Englishman his quietus. (See sketch at chapter heading.)

What's happened to the fellow? He has disappeared! Eschwege searches the landscape once more. No sign of him!

He can certainly never find him if he has landed down in the reeds with a disabled engine. The upper wing surface of the B.E. is painted dark brown, so that it will be hardly recognizable in this part of the world. (Photograph 22.)

Eschwege flies home in the dumps. He has fired six hundred rounds. The Tommy is finished off— but how to prove it?

Can't be done, unfortunately.

.   .   .   .   .

Not until after the lapse of five weeks did we obtain the definite news we desired. It was given us by an English airman whom the Bulgarians had shot down. He stated:

"The B.E. 2D 90 h.p. was attacked over Porna by a German scout. The machine sustained more than 200 hits and made a forced landing on bad ground to westward of the Takhino marsh. The stick, tank, engine, instruments, struts, spars, wheels and propeller were so riddled that the machine had to be scrapped. The pilot received four wounds."

II

Misfortunes seldom come singly.

Eschwege had a similar piece of bad luck two days after the aforesaid encounter. When flying a barrage patrol, he sighted a B.E. one-seater over Lake Takhino and promptly attacked it. After a brief engagement the Englishman sheered off and made for the further shore. When Eschwege sat on his neck, he extricated himself by an extraordinarily daring nose-dive and landed at Monuhi aerodrome.

. . . . .

In this case, too, we obtained supplementary news concerning the " How ? " from a similar source of information, and this time we even received enlightenment on the " Who's Who ? " Eschwege's opponent was Captain Green in person ; after his machine has sustained sixteen hits, a jammed gun forced him to break off the combat. We laughed with malicious glee when we heard the news, and even Eschwege's face showed his satisfaction.

" I always wanted to get Green in my sights," he said. " According to that Englishman's statement, he has already shot down four German machines. But I'm certain that gun jam is a bit of an exaggeration. The good fellow was simply in a tight corner."

III

Like all good things, all bad ones are three.

Neither of those two successful encounters could be credited as " victories " because the machines did not fall into our hands and there were no ground witnesses to testify. Poor Eschwege had no better luck in his third affair.

As it demonstrates the difficulties which had to be overcome before an opponent shot down on the farther side of the lines could be credited to his vanquisher, I propose to let the official documents speak for themselves.

The Staffel's combat report of March 8th, 1917:

Scout machine : Lieut. von Eschwege. Duration

of patrol 10.15 a.m.—11.10 a.m.   Took off in pursuit
of enemy two-seater.   After an indecisive combat the
enemy aircraft escaped across Lake Takhino, flying at
200 metres.

Bulgarian official communiqué, March 9th, 1917 :
    " After an air fight over Seres an enemy aircraft
was forced to land behind the enemy's lines."

Reply to our inquiry by the 10th Bulgarian Division :
    " The forced landing was definitely seen by the
    Bulgarian observation posts.   Moreover, a metal
    part was detached from the machine during the
    fight and came down near Alistrati."

Telegram to the German staff officer attached to
G.H.Q., 2nd Bulgarian Army Corps :
    " Please obtain and forward metal part."

The examination of the metal part showed that it
was actually a part shot away from the engine.   It
appeared to belong to a vertical push rod.

Statement by a R.N.A.S. airman, who was taken
prisoner :
    " On March 8th one of our machines had a fight
    with the scout from Drama.   The observer was
    wounded in the hip.   The machine made a forced
    landing.   It was badly damaged."

Statement by a R.F.C. airman, who was taken
prisoner :
    " At the beginning of March one of our Nieuports
    sustained much damage, including an oblique hit on
    the undercarriage strut, so that the undercarriage
    broke off when the machine made a forced landing.
    The machine was smashed up.   Moreover, it
    sustained so many hits that it had to be scrapped as
    totally unserviceable.   The observer was severely
    wounded in the lungs, but recovered."

·   ·   ·   ·   ·

With us a victory did not count as such until it was won and confirmed.

This fact Lieutenant Becher, an observer ace from Hudova, who was transferred to my Staffel, learnt to his cost. With his thirty-two years he was the eldest of us all, and his predilection for fat cigars earned him the nickname of " the alderman."

When he was still serving in the Vardar sector, he fell in with a group of ten Sopwiths on his return from a photographic flight and damaged the engine of one of them so badly that the pilot was forced to land on our side of the lines. But then came his bad luck. Lieutenant Pocock, the English pilot, was not taken prisoner until he had burnt his machine.

When we hailed our comrade as the victor of the aerial battle, Mr. Pocock said with a smile :

" What ? You shot me down ? Not a bit of it ! I didn't even see any German airmen, let alone fight them ! "

But Becher was not the man to abandon a good cause without a struggle. With the assistance of the works master he extricated the engine from the debris, and lo ! he found not only several bullet holes but even some fragments of machine-gun bullets. Nevertheless, Pocock persisted in his denial.

" Yes, those hits are from another fight which I had a couple of weeks ago."

The consequence was that the Kogenluft authorities did not credit our man with the victory. It was a bitter blow for him, but it shows how superconscientiously our victory lists were made out.

But for that very reason Becher received greater credit from those same authorities when he located the big net barrage in Salonica harbour. His photographs were most welcome to the Admiralty staff because they furnished a basis for submarine operations.

Becher had also many tough fights to survive when he worked with us.   He also lived up to his reputation as a photographic ace.   Like his deeds he did not lack recognition while he was with us.

When the congratulatory telegram which had gone the round of our table came back to me, I was particularly delighted with the " B " with which the " alderman " had countersigned it.

23. ABOVE THE CLOUDS

24. BELOW THE CLOUDS

25. MACEDONIAN ROAD AFTER HEAVY RAIN

26. GREEK MOUNTAIN LANDSCAPE

27. MONASTIR

CHAPTER XI

WINDS AND CLOUDS

THE cloud formations in the Balkans were quite incalculable. (Photograph 23.)

Once Wethekam and I landed on the Bulgarian aerodrome at Belisa after a front patrol, because I had received a summons to the H.Q. of the 2nd Bulgarian army. The sky clouded over in the afternoon, so that I was anxious to get off, although our Bulgarian comrades of the air gave us a hearty invitation to spend the night with them. Wethekam tried his

machine-gun before we started and had the misfortune
to put several bullets through the wood of a propeller
blade.   A Bulgarian lieutenant raised his index finger
in serious warning.

"Better stay here !   Losch prisnak ! " (Bad omen !)

I could not help laughing.   In addition to obtaining
their machines from us, the Bulgarian airmen also
took over the superstitions to which all of us—myself
unfortunately not excepted—were foolish slaves.   I
would only fly in the old crash helmet I had worn
ever since my first flight—I never allowed myself to
be photographed before I took off—I never looked at
a machine which had been shot down in flames—I did
not wish a comrade " Good luck ! " before he took
off, but " Hals und Beinbruch ! " (May you break your
neck and your limbs !)—I swore by my lucky numbers,
7, 3, 5 and 13—and I. . . .

As, however, I would rather have died than con-
fessed my own superstitions to the Bulgarians, I felt
unwilling to let them detain me.   It would have been
all right if I had decided to stay of my own free will,
but under the circumstances it was impossible for me
to yield.

I therefore said " Mnogo blagodarja ! " (Many
thanks !) and " Do wischdane ! " (Au revoir !)   Then
Wethekam and I whirled off.

We were just able to clear the 1,700 metres of the
summits of the Pirin range, but thick clouds had
collected round Mount Rhodope, where a gale tossed
them about at terrific speed.   A few minutes later
we found our way to Drama barred by a huge thunderstorm, which filled the valley.   If we thrust our way
into it, we risked being struck by lightning or colliding
with a rocky cliff—two most unpleasant possibilities.
Likewise I had no desire to risk a forced landing in

that most unalluring valley, for the Kofl had sent a telegram round to all aerodromes a few weeks previously :

"Crashes must be avoided at all costs as no replacement machines in park."

Of course, Eschwege must encounter a gust after taking off on the following day, with the result that he cracked off his undercarriage. If I should happen to crash a machine on top of that, I saw ourselves becoming most unpleasantly conspicuous. I therefore preferred to take a bite of my sour apple and fly back to our Bulgarian friends at Belisa, even at the risk of being welcomed with a series of knowing grins. So right about turn !

Wethekam put his machine obediently into the turn which would set us on our way back. But meanwhile the clouds had dropped so low about Mount Pirin that we were encircled on all sides and could only buzz round like a cockchafer under a glass bowl. (Photograph 24.)

So there was nothing left for us but a forced landing. After a long search we discovered a maize field which had been reaped. It certainly contained a number of deep furrows, in which all too many thick beheaded stalks still stood up about a foot high ; as, moreover, the wind's direction was at an angle to the lines of these furrows, we had an excellent chance of cracking off our undercarriage when we landed. Even if we had the luck to escape this sad fate, it looked as if, at least, the propeller would be splintered when it touched the maize stalks. But we had to go down, because the clouds were sinking lower and lower, thus literally forcing us down to earth. I bade Wethekam cut his engine and gave him instructions.

" Take your time over the flattening out ; then pancake so that we taxi the shortest possible distance. Above all, keep your tail down, so as to prevent the machine turning turtle and the prop going to smithereens ! "

Wethekam nodded, and then proceeded to do his job faultlessly. The furrows gave our undercarriage a bad jolting in spite of its rubber springs, but as we had only little way on us, we escaped with several bumps. Then we came to a standstill.

From the nearby town of Nevrokop I rang up Eschwege in order to stop our people worrying about us. But meanwhile the thunderstorm had raged itself out in a heavy downpour and disappeared as quickly as it came. The evening sun evolved a magnificent rainbow over the valley. For the moment, however, we regarded this message of peace as merely an irony because we were faced with the prospect of a difficult take off from the hard field of maize stubble. Wethekam had meanwhile inquired whether there was any better starting ground in the neighbourhood, but as a matter of fact, we had come down instinctively on the only spot of ground where we had any possible chance of avoiding a smash.

A number of Bulgarians from the little town had wandered out to stare at our machine. I put three sturdy fellows under its tail and gave them instructions :

" Nepodwischno dörschö, do snak ! " (Hold on until I give the word.)

With their assistance I hoped to bring up the engine's revs to a figure which would ensure us the minimum stretch of taxying. My arrangements proved to be the right ones ; after two or three wild leaps, Wethekam was able to lift the machine. But

she still had too little way on her and tried to sideslip ;
he therefore let her go down again a bit and then
climbed up afresh in an elegant " ladder-start."

We waved our gratitude to our helpers, and half-an-
hour later we made a good landing in Drama.

.   .   .   .   .

The clouds were not our only troubles ; often
enough the rain could make itself most unpleasant.
Even in Drama the streets became gaily babbling
brooks in rainy weather. (Photograph 25.) In
treeless Macedonia downpours flow away very quickly.
The beds of the rivers and streams cannot contain the
masses of water that descend into them from all
directions, and so overflow their banks. The flood
whirls along so violently and so unexpectedly that
men and beasts are often drowned in the narrow
valleys. But the aerodromes were mostly located in
barren mountain country, where there was little
agriculture (photograph 26), so that only the valleys
were practicable as sites for them, even though the
danger of flood was twice as great there.

.   .   .   .   .

Certainly we often longed for clouds and rain with
all our hearts, when the spells of fine weather
continued too long. We rejoiced at a visit from the
clouds like children welcoming a favourite uncle.
If we had the bad luck to find much activity at the
front when these periods of " blessed weather "
came, we cursed heartily, but flew all the same—not
because we were under orders to do so, but because
of our comradeship with the infantry.

There was splendid photographic weather after the
rain. As the drops washed down all the dust in the

air, even oblique photos were most successful, as
may be seen by an example from the photography of
Section 38.   (Photograph 27.)

.   .   .   .   .

I can sleep in any situation—on a cupboard, in the
rack of a railway carriage, standing in a corner, on a
march—yes, even with a bad conscience.   But the
English heavy bombs, which their airmen were
wont to drop on our aerodrome by night, made such
a row that they would have even roused a person in a
trance, and also " the wind, the wind, that heavenly
child," showed itself to be such a full-grown hooligan
in this part of the world that it always jerked us all
speedily on to our feet.

In this fashion I was snatched from my sleep one
night by a wild clatter.   I sat up and listened in the
darkness.   A hurricane was raging through the alleys
of the little town and tearing the tiles off the roofs.
When I tried to ascertain the cause of the clatter, I
discovered that the wind had wrenched a window from
its hinges and smashed it.   I looked at my watch ;
the time was just before midnight.

I grew worried about my tents.   They had suffered
severely from wind and weather—would they stand
firm ?   It was no great matter if the storm tore pieces
out of them, because we could patch them up again,
but if the wind reached our machines, its full force
would catch them under the wings and pound them
to shapeless masses.   I grabbed at the telephone to
make inquiries, but received no answer.   The connection was broken.   So out I had to go !

I dressed quickly and allowed the gale to blow me
out to the aerodrome.   On the way I met one of my
men, who had been sent to fetch me.

" Carry on and warn all officers and men living in the town," I instructed him.

I arrived only just in time. The men in charge of the machines had divided themselves into groups for each tent and were holding on to the ropes on the luff side.

I came to a decision : if the gale ripped up a tent or blew it down, the mass of poles and canvas would be bound to smash the machines. So we rolled them out and anchored them in the open, with their noses turned to the wind. It was high time, for the canvas of a tent split open just before we could push the last two-seater out.

Although we all gave a hand, we were overpowered by the force of the raging storm which hurled the tent down. But we had some luck in the midst of our misfortunes ; although every spar in the right upper wing was broken and only a shred remained of the aileron, the rest of the damage was so negligible that the machine was able to be repaired in the aircraft park.

Hour after hour went by in the course of our struggle against the forces of nature. The grey dawn came, but still there was no abatement. Shortly before sunrise another tent went to the devil. Good for us that we had pulled the machines outside ! Their bracing-wires howled in the storm as though in a nosedive.

At last, at last, about 4 a.m. the hurricane began to abate. We were happy to find it had left us victors, although suffering from some slight damage. (Photograph 28.)

.   .   .   .   .

There was also an alleviating balm for these sorrows.

The next time we welcomed a captive English airman at our table, he told us that the storm had also destroyed two tents at Badimal aerodrome that night —and the two aeroplanes inside them as well. We laughed heartily at this proof of our link with the English airmen that Nature had given us.

Sorrow shared is sorrow halved !

.   .   .   .   .

I was on the way home to Drama, with Kuhlo at the stick. We had only to cross the Boz Dagh, and then all was plain sailing. Although the ridge of this mountain was covered with high clouds, which we could not climb above, we knew the peak well enough from former experience and knew, also, that its saddles were not buried too deeply. We had to get home in any case, because we had not much petrol left, and a forced landing in the mountains was bound to mean a smashed machine. So we risked it and groped our way into the clouds. Luckily, they were thin enough to justify the risk. Often enough we literally brushed the tops of the trees with our wheels, but we got away with it.

We breathed freely with the relief, for after crossing the ridge we found the clouds grow lighter. A backward glance sighted clear sky ; the clouds had only anchored themselves on the upper parts of the mountains. Kuhlo, therefore, opened his throttle a bit, so that after a few minutes we found ourselves free of all but the last shreds of cloud.

We were already over the valley through which the Lisa-Sevindria flows. It was a narrow enough gorge, lined with jagged walls of rock, but farther down it grew wider, giving us a distant greeting from the houses of Drama. (Photograph 29.)

28. A TENT AFTER THE STORM

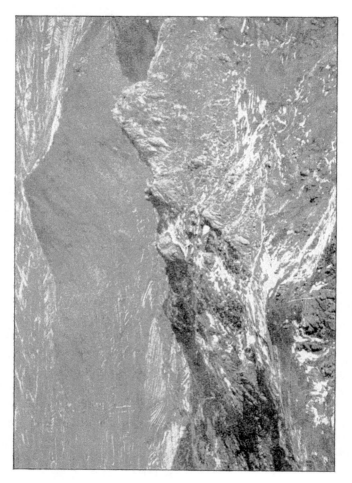

29. MOUNTAIN LANDSCAPE

But our joy was destined to be shortlived, for now we ran into a real mess of nasty weather. The strong side-wind was broken by the bluffs of the ranges on either side of the valley, and united with the warm air-currents rising from below to form eddies of a positively grotesque ferocity. We had the feeling that we had blundered into a host of unchained demons and could also imagine we felt their physical presence. We heard their inexorable will to destroy us echoed in their screeching war-cries and panting gusts of breath. We ducked when they assailed us with their fists and clubs, but although we had to be prepared for them to smash a wing or the steering surfaces in one of their furious onslaughts, we took our precautions with cold hearts and sullen anger.

One giant seized the front of our machine and made it rear up like a shying horse. Scarcely had Kuhlo parried this attack by putting the stick down before we blundered into an airpocket, so that the machine threatened to drop headforemost into the depths. The camera and plate-sheaths slid from their holders and banged against the wooden floor of the cockpit.

When I tried to bend over to retrieve them, I was unexpectedly thumped against the side. An eddy had pushed itself under the right wing and tried to tip us over. I had hardly time to stow the heavy camera case away and make it fast with some wire before a mighty shove hurled us round, so that our nose faced eastward.

While Kuhlo was putting the machine back into her former course by dint of gentle persistence, we went down with such a mighty flop that the butt of the machine-gun was wrenched from its powerful holder and banged against my head. My good old crash

I

helmet tempered the force of the blow, but my cranium buzzed as I forced the butt back into position and secured it with an isolation band. But before I could finish the job, a fresh gust pitched us so far over on to one side that I made an alarmed clutch at a side of the cockpit.

A full ammunition drum rolled out of its holder and fell on to my toes. I wedged it between my feet instinctively, and it was well for me that I did so, for just as I tried to bend down to pick it up, a descending gust pushed our tail down so hard that the plate-sheaths slid away to the back end of the cockpit. If the heavy drum had followed them, it would have made our machine tail-heavy and probably jammed the control wire as well. Whether Kuhlo could have then brought the machine back on to an even keel, seems to me doubtful, to say the least of it. But as it was, we had a piece of good luck mixed in with the bad.

Slowly, infinitely slowly, our little town drew nearer.

I took the precaution of buckling my body-belt round me, as we were not expecting any fights. But a monster of a gust charged us so brutally, soon after I had closed the catch that I was thrown forward unexpectedly. The stout belt-holders tore like paper ; I went down on my knees and hung on desperately to the framework. Luckily, my hands maintained a better hold than the hemp did.

The storm giants seemed to exhaust their strength with this last violent action. The valley grew wider, so that the wind had more scope for a smooth passage through. We certainly sustained a few more hard knocks occasionally, but after the experiences of the last quarter of an hour we took them in our stride.

We made a good landing, and as we were climbing out of the machine, I bestowed a grin of pleasure on Kuhlo.

" That was a tough time ! " I remarked.

But meanwhile Eschwege had arrived and was examining the machine. " Not a thing smashed ! You've had the devil's own luck, my lad." Then he turned to me. " I got into just such a witches' cauldron not long before you took over," he said.

" I was supposed to be testing a two-seater which had a new engine built into it, and so I took the mechanic up with me. The machine ran into a downward gust and flopped down on her nose. I just managed to get her under control again, but I'd had enough, and so I landed as quick as I could. When I was taxying, I called out to the chap behind me : " Man alive, we've been dam' lucky ! " But as I got no answer, I looked round, and to my astonishment the observer's seat was empty. The poor fellow had been pitched out from about a thousand metres up ! " (See sketch at chapter heading.)

With silent, pensive melancholy I thought of the fresco on the wall of Flying Section 38's mess, which depicts a much happier version of such a crash. (Photograph 30.)

CHAPTER XII

OUR FRIENDS THE BULGARIANS

OUR friends the Bulgarians !
There was an unpleasant side to the Bulgarians as well as to the Turks. Since evil communications corrupt good manners, they fired at their own side's airmen on most unsuitable occasions. At least, however, they were not quite as consistent as the Turks, because they only fired on us every now and then, whereas the latter peppered every machine within range.

We generally flew low over our own troops when returning from the front, because we glided back to the home aerodrome. As, moreover, our Bulgarian allies were excellent marksmen, we often found ourselves in tight corners. Once they brought Siebold and myself down with two very neat hits.

Our huge Maltese crosses were easily recognizable, and our star-signals could hardly be overlooked. But anyone who has tasted the joys of hunting knows how dominating this passion can be with certain people.

Unfortunately the Bulgarian Archie-gunners had a most regrettable psychical defect. They suffered severely from chronic loss of memory, for no matter how often we complained, they could never recollect a single instance of having fired at us. So we had no alternative save to seek consolation in philosophy.

Firstly : They fired at the English as well as at us—and with even greater success, as we knew by the many men and machines they hauled down.

And secondly : They did not only fire on German and English machines. They peppered their own Bulgarian ones as well. So when Major Popkristeff had to report once more :

" Close reconnaissance broken off because of heavy fire from own batteries, in spite of repeated signals."

we laughed heartily and made our reconciliation.

Rawno prawo sa fssitchki ! (Equal rights for all !)

.   .   .   .   .

In other respects the Bulgarians—from the voynik (private soldier) up to the glawnokommandujusch (commander-in-chief), General Jekoff, were the best comrades one could have desired.

The nearest to our hearts were, naturally, the Bulgarian airmen belonging to the sections commanded by Popkristeff and Bogdanoff. Two of their officers accomplished a real cavalryman's feat when they managed to recross the English trenches after a forced landing behind the enemy's lines. The following is their actual report :

REPORT

on flying operations in night hours of May 23rd—24th, 1918. Orders : to bomb and attack with machine-gun fire English establishments in the area between Gümüsdere and Lake Takhino.

Operations : 25-kg. bombs in Gümüsdere Valley, $12\frac{1}{2}$-kg. on Kopriva station, $12\frac{1}{2}$ on the station to the north of Dragitshevo, 25-kg. on Orljak camp. Attacked camps and stations between Orljak and Lake Takhino with machine-gun fire, descending to 400 metres over Gorasanli station and illuminating objective with star shells.

On the return flight one cylinder failed, and then the engine went dead. Nevertheless, we succeeded in landing on marshy ground on the flooded left bank of the Struma, where our machine was half submerged in the morass.

We broke up the machine and its gun, and strewed all the parts in the water. We refrained from burning the machine (an English two-seater captured at Demirhissar) for the following reasons :

(1) It was completely unserviceable.

(2) It was impossible to salve it.

(3) The flames would have drawn the attention of the enemy to our presence, so that it would have been impossible for us to make our way back through the marsh and thick bush.

With guidance from our compass we marched in a north-east direction during the night and slunk through the cordon of enemy pickets at dawn, reaching our own outposts about 12 (noon).

Lieut. Usunoff,	Lieut. Pop Atasanoff,
Pilot.	Observer

of the Bulgarian Flying Section 1.

. . . . .

As the Bulgarians possessed no scout machines at that time, Lieutenant Balan, who thirsted after daring deeds, had the cockades of a captured Nieuport painted out and replaced by crosses. When he did not achieve the desired victory in this machine, he came to a quick decision to go out with an observer in an ordinary two-seater and hunt the English. Although no working machine attached to our Staffel ever succeeded in obtaining official confirmation of a victory, the efficient Balan contrived to bring down his first Englishman in this fashion. By virtue of the "law of series" his section commander, Major Popkristeff, then succeeded in performing a similar feat when flying with Lieutenant Ivanoff. And Captain Milanoff brought their total up to three, when he obtained a scout machine.

. . . . .

We were also in close touch with other Bulgarian troops. The staff of the 10th Bulgarian Division were quartered in Drama, and I had to report daily to their chief, our dear Lieutenant-Colonel Asmanoff. I shall never forget what he did for us and how he always treated us as his equals in age and seniority.

The Bulgarians knew how to appreciate the facts that we dropped big fat bombs, made good reconnaissances and brought back clear photos. But this respect for us was a light matter in comparison with the love and admiration they lavished on our Rudi von Eschwege. We could well understand this, because we cherished similar feelings. They were always thoroughly delighted when we could show them one captured English machine after another—burnt, wrecked, or intact, as the case might be. Moreover their vanity was just as flattered as ours by the fact that the English were so strongly influenced by Eschwege's victories that their airmen grew continually more and more cautious, until at last they only ventured over Drama at a very great height by daylight.

* * * * *

One day I received a visit from Lieutenant Kerikoff, the orderly officer attached to the divisional staff.

" We have a request to make," he said. " Lieutenant-Colonel Trifonoff, the group-leader of our 7th Artillery Regiment, would like to inspect the positions of his batteries south of Seres from the air."

" Can he use a machine-gun ? "

" A bit ! "

I considered the matter. " Good ! Tell him to be on the aerodrome at 6 a.m. to-morrow. Sergeant Stattaus will take him up, and I'll give him Corporal van Ahlen's Roland as an escort as well."

Kerikoff expressed his thanks and departed.

* * * * *

The two machines took off at 6.15 a.m. the following morning. (See sketch at chapter heading.)

The observation machine circled round over the battery positions at a height of 1,000 metres, with the scout above it. When the Bulgarian officer had seen everything, Stattaus headed for Drama again. Ahlen scoured the air over the front once more and then followed behind and above the observation machine, having observed no enemy aircraft. Like Stattaus, he was glad to see this ticklish business completed without any incidents.

But one should never praise a day before nightfall nor a flight before its landing. They see two machines heading for them. Germans ? Impossible ! The only other machine to take off from Drama this morning is the one in which Corporal Hommola is piloting Lieutenant König on a long distance reconnaissance. So they must be English !

And now the two are near enough for Ahlen to make out the type. English B.E.s ! So it is up to him to anticipate them before they can attack the two-seater. A fight might have unpleasant consequences for the Bulgarian colonel, who is quite inexperienced in aerial warfare, as well as for our Stattaus, who is thus left with insufficient protection for his back.

As the Englishmen have not yet sighted the scout, which is flying 800 metres above the two-seater, they head for the latter. Ahlen's mind is quickly made up ; he puts his nose down for a dive on the surprised opponents and is lucky enough to come out on the tail of one of them. The enemy turns off towards the lines to get away from his burst, but Ahlen follows him, shooting as he turns. Then the other Englishman leaves the German two-seater in order to assist his comrade.

When Ahlen hears the English machine-gun rattling away behind him, he pulls his machine sharply round to engage this new opponent. As far as he can ascertain by a quick glance, Stattaus is going nose-down for Drama.

So his job is to keep the two English machines

busy and prevent them from following the Albatros.
A skilfully-executed turn puts one of them in his burst.
He must have hit him several times, because he does
not try to fight—he even does not attack Ahlen when
the latter has to break away to deal with the assaults
of his companion.

He contrives to get away from the second Englishman's burst by a steep turn.   With a joyful eye he
sees the first Englishman flying back across the lines.
He has certainly sustained some damage, for otherwise
he would not leave his comrade in the lurch.

A quick glance round.   Stattaus has gained such a
good start that he is hardly visible.

Ahlen breathes a sigh of relief.   His job is done !
And then another burst rattles into his machine. . . .

.   .   .   .   .

One machine was returning as I reached the aerodrome.   I looked at the time : 7.25 a.m.   So it must
be König, I decided, as he had been in the air since
5.30 a.m.   But as soon as the machine came near, I
saw to my astonishment that I was mistaken.   It was
Stattaus, with the Bulgarian colonel.

" Where's Ahlen ? " I asked.

Stattaus told me the little he knew.   Hm, then
he'll arrive later, I thought.   Minutes passed, but
Ahlen did not appear.

At last, nearly half an hour later, we heard the
drone of an engine from the direction of the front.
And then a machine loomed up out of the morning
sky.   I put my glasses to my eyes.   It was a two-seater
i.e., König and Hommola.

.   .   .   .   .

But what has happened to Ahlen ?

When the Englishman he has damaged clears off, he has only one opponent to worry about. That is a better game than fighting two, one of whom will be always sitting on his back.

They circle round one another in an exciting battle of turns. Ahlen comes into the Englishman's burst once more ; above the roar of the engine he hears the hard metallic thud. A hit ! And the next moment the hand of the pressure gauge begins to drop. Tank holed !

Ahlen switches on to the gravity tank, and puts new life into the weary revolutions of his propeller. Slowly the Roland raises her nose.

But the Englishman has not let his respite pass unused. Once again Ahlen is in his burst ; once again his bullets rattle against the engine ; once again the hand drops back. At the same instant Ahlen becomes aware of a strong odour of petrol. A thin spray spurts into his face and smears his goggles. He pulls them down instinctively and gives an upward glance. The petrol pipe connecting with the gravity tank has been punctured. A twist—shut off —the engine will get no more petrol now—it gives a few rumbles—then it goes dead. So down and land !

Luckily they are not in the mountains but over the plain. But even here the consequence will be a forced landing on unknown territory, with trenches that will make it no pleasant affair, especially if he has to bring it off under the fire of a resolute opponent.

Ahlen pushes his machine down in a nose-dive to get out of the enemy's burst at least, and looks around for a suitable landing place. Ah, that spot will do ! So now he catches the machine again—what a long time she seems to take to flatten out—puts her down with a jolt—a short taxi—then she comes to a stand-still in long grass. Ahlen unbuckles his safety-belt in the twinkling of an eye and jumps out of his seat.

A few paces to his left he spies a ditch, in which he throws himself full length. High time, too! The B.E., which has been following hard upon him, approaches his machine in a glide to finish it off. After rattling the contents of a drum down on to this convenient ground target, the pilot puts his machine into a climb and flies homeward across Lake Takhino. Ahlen creeps joyfully from his ditch and examines the Roland.

The Englishman's aim was excellent during the fight, but he appears to have had little practice on ground targets, for he has failed to score a single hit on this one.

·　　·　　·　　·　　·

Meanwhile, I was running about the aerodrome in a worried frame of mind. At last, about 9 a.m., Angeloff came from the telephone with sad news:

"Report from the front. After fight with two Englishmen German machine forced to land near Tschiftl Tefik Bey, eight kilometres south-east of Seres."

"Yes, go on! Pilot wounded? Machine damaged?"

Angeloff shrugged his shoulders. "They don't know. They could only watch from a long distance away."

I considered the matter. If Ahlen could not take off again, it would be hours before fuller details came to hand. So nothing to do but wait! After pacing up and down the aerodrome several times, I saw Angeloff approaching me again.

" An Englishman dropped two heavy bombs on the German machine which landed."

" Did he hit it ? "

Once more Angeloff shrugged his shoulders.

" They don't know. They could only watch from a long distance away."

I decided to remain on the aerodrome until a sensible report came along and gave me an opportunity to act. About 10 a.m. Angeloff stumped along once more, but this time he arrived with a joyful face, which led me to hope for good news.

" English aircraft—two this time—dropped bombs on our machine. It was completely destroyed, but the pilot is unhurt."

I drew a deep breath. A pity about the machine and the work it would entail to recover it from such a Godforsaken hole, but the main thing was that our Ahlen remained undamaged. I sent word at once to Lieutenant-Colonel Trifonoff, who rang up once an hour to inquire whether there was any news of his valiant protector.

Then I went into the town. But I was hardly off the aerodrome before I heard the drone of an engine coming from the direction of the front. A narrow smudge was approaching, but no other machine of ours was up. So it could only be an English one! But by the sound of the engine it was a German— most mysterious !

And now I could make out a Maltese cross. So it really was a German ! Could perhaps a machine from Hudova have got into trouble on a long distance reconnaissance to Salonica and be wanting to land on our aerodrome ? Possible—indeed, most probable !

I scurried back to the aerodrome, arriving just in

time to welcome the man who climbed out of the machine—Ahlen !

I glowed with pleasure as he approached me and reported himself back from his patrol. I shook his hand emotionally.

" But how is this possible ? Not long ago we received news that your machine was destroyed by English bombs ? "

Ahlen laughed.

" Yes, sir, you've had some practice at bombing machines in the Takhino marshes. The Englishmen came along twice and put six heavy bombs down on my machine—or rather, in the neighbourhood of my machine. But luckily, they didn't hit it ! "

" But you made a forced landing ? Wasn't your engine hit in the fight ? "

" Yes. Main tank and leads to gravity tank hit. But I managed to patch up the leads."

" Now you see how good my instructions were. Always take an isolation band with you."

" I'm sorry to say I forgot it." Ahlen rolled up the sleeve of his tunic. " But I had a leucoplast strip on my old wound. I took it off and patched up the two ends of the petrol lead with it." I shook his hand again in warm appreciation.

" When you tell that tale later to someone," I said, " He'll reply : ' My boy, you're a damn fine liar ! ' But I've seen with my own eyes that it's the truth, and so I can only whisper ' Damn well done ! ' ' "

CHAPTER XIII

HOSTILE ALLIES

A TELEPHONE message came through from the 2nd Bulgarian Army H.Q.

" Staffel-leaders report at H.Q. for conference."

We liked invitations of that sort, because we landed at Belisa aerodrome, where the commander of the

1st Bulgarian Flying Section, Major Popkristeff, always welcomed us with hearty hospitality.

" Well, Siebold," I said, " what about it ?   Shall we go there together ?   We can take off early in the morning and do a bit of a reconnaissance first."

Siebold laughed.   " O.K. for me ! "

.   .   .   .   .

The next morning.   We have flown our bit and are now swinging over the Bulgarian trenches. Before us looms up slowly the Rupel Pass, where the Struma breaks through the foothills and flows into the plain.   I search the sky once more for English aircraft. The air is free of them.   The tension, which sharpens the senses and braces the nerves when one is flying in enemy country, is relaxed.   I sit down and write my report, so that I can send it off to Drama as soon as we land.   Then I am a free man for the rest of the day.   Lieutenant König rules in Drama now, and I can rely on him.   And then—crack !

I start up with the shock and must make a hasty clutch at the side of the cockpit, for Siebold has put the machine into a steep turn.   A few seconds later the black smoke of a bursting shell floats past on our right.   Well ?   Not one Archie potted us when we were across the lines—and now the English must needs send a farewell greeting after us !   Certainly we are low enough—the altimeter records a bare 1,200. I cast a searching look behind me.

And again :   " Crack ! "   This time the burst is close behind us.   The report is sharper than the first one—so the second shell is better placed.   Siebold puts the machine into a series of irregular turns to make the target harder for the Tommies over yonder, and I strain my eyes to scour the ground behind me.

These English batteries which are giving us a

30. A FRESCO ON OUR MESS WALL

31. ANTI-AIRCRAFT FIRE

headache some good few kilometres behind our own
lines must have a very long range. I take off my hat
to the lads who can put us in a nasty hole at this
distance! But where are their guns then? Eagerly
I scan the terrain beyond the trenches in order to
locate them by their flashes.

Hallo—a flash! But not behind us—no, right
below us! So we are being potted by our own side,
by a Bulgarian battery! That's why those shell-
bursts are so splendidly aimed.

I look at the map. Naturally, it is the notorious
Archies of Demirhissar again!

A mild attack of goose-flesh comes over me as I
think of that ghastly quarter of an hour on the Western
front when I was dazzled by the German searchlights
on my return one night and bracketed by German
Archies.

Out with my Very pistol, into which I put a star-
cartridge! There we are again—" Crack!" The
shell that went off from the flash I spotted just now has
burst. But luckily, far away to the right this time,
thank Heaven!

I fire my signal. Siebold starts and turns towards
me when he hears the sharp report so close to him.
He nods appeasedly when I show him the pistol.
The white bullet whizzes through the air in a long
arc and bursts into white stars with a gentle report.
The stars sink slowly earthwards, leaving trails of
silvery smoke behind them. They signify: " Look
out! We're German airmen! " I quickly fire off
another signal after them. (See sketch at chapter
heading.)

But the Bulgarians are as little influenced by my
signals as the Germans were that night in the Champagne. Again and again I repeat my signs of

K

recognition. In vain! Shells and shrapnels fly up towards us in pretty alternation. In the midst of all my perils the thing which rankles most is the fact that the Tommies over yonder can watch the attentions our allies are giving us.

By putting the machine's nose well down, Siebold extracts from it a speed of over two hundred kilometres an hour, so that every second is carrying us fifty metres and every minute three kilometres away from the unfriendly Bulgarian battery. Moreover, he zigzags at irregular intervals in order to make the target more difficult for the gunners down below.

Meanwhile I fire off one signal after another, but they are wasted on these glupetz (idiots). But I must see to it that the other Archies do not join in. By our steep dive we have lost considerable height and are now only about eight hundred metres above the level of the valley. The advantage of that is that the men below can recognize our crosses with the naked eye.

Now there is a pause in the shooting. Have they spotted us as Germans at last? Or have we passed, happily, out of the range of this hellish battery? I cast a glance of relief behind me—and then—damn it all!—there's another flash down below there. Anxious moments of suspense—ten seconds—twenty —thirty—forty—a dud? Or have my eyes deceived me?

" Crack ! " The shell bursts so close in front of us that for a second we are flying through the stinking haze of its explosion-cloud. At the same moment I hear a thud in the engine—a hit! That into the bargain !

The startled Siebold bends forward and puts the machine into a horizontal position. But there seems to be no trouble, for the rev-counter continues to mark 1,600. Our hopes are illusive, however, for a few seconds later the hand drops back to 800 and the engine begins to sputter. So it has been hit on some vital spot.

A look down. We have flown past the neck of the Rupel Pass, and the valley is spreading out. But there is still no place for a forced landing ; all sorts of perils await us if we go down there. Our beautiful new Albatros is bound to be smashed up unless we have extraordinary luck, but in any case we shall have to look out for a landing-spot somewhere. The only possible chance seems to be a landing on a bank of scree in the river-bed.

Although Siebold is no longer pushing the machine down, we still continually lose height. I cast a mistrustful glance over his shoulder at the rev-counter. It seems to be in a better mood and hovers between 1,200 and 1,400. It is impossible for us to ascertain the damage done by that shell splinter at present, but apparently only one cylinder is out of action. There is, however, the danger of its piston pitting itself and bringing the engine to a standstill.

Nevertheless we begin to hope again. If the engine will hold out for a time we can, perhaps, reach the Bulgarian aerodrome in a prolonged glide. How lovely that would be !

Meanwhile the hostile Bulgarian battery has ceased fire. Either we are now out of range or masked by the mountains which flank the pass. In any case, we need expect no further trouble from that direction. Heaven grant that no more ambitious gunners get wild notions into their heads and open fire ! A direct hit would be so easy at our low height.

Slowly, infinitely slowly, the landscape glides away

beneath us. Now the little houses and garden plots of the Bulgarian headquarters in Sv. Bratsch gleam up to us—now we have flown past them—and at last, at last—though still far ahead—the tents on the Bulgarian aerodrome greet us in friendly welcome.

Shall we do it ? We are only 300 metres up. The aerodrome creeps slowly nearer. Then—the engine begins to sputter again—the hand of the rev-counter sways restlessly leftward—and then comes to a standstill at 800. That means that a whole block of three cylinders has gone on strike. Siebold casts a quick glance ahead ; he cannot keep the engine going much longer. He throttles down a few pegs to ease the strain on it.

Long, anxious moments !

Deeper and deeper we drop. But at last we are quite close to the landing ground. Our Bulgarian comrades stand down below, waving up to us, while a squad is busy laying out the landing mark. We wave back joyfully.

Then Siebold goes into a glide—and promptly— he was not a moment too soon—the propeller goes dead. Can we do it ? Or shall we hurtle on to the slope falling away to southward from the end of the aerodrome ? To-day we cannot allow ourselves the luxury of a flight round the place if we overshoot the mark and fail in our first attempt to land. And we can also gain no help from a few pegs of gas to-day if our glide brings us down too short.

But everything goes off well—we land—taxi— come to a full stop.

Done it !

. . . . .

The Bulgarian airmen shake hands with us when we have leapt joyfully from our machine.

"Dobr den! Kakste?" (God day! How are you?)

"Polowina i polowina!" (Half and half!)

Then we have a look at the damage. A shell splinter has knocked the rocker-arm off one exhaust valve, and another has gone through our right wheel.

Siebold bends down to whisper in my ear. "Man alive, wouldn't it be great to put a star shell in the tummy of that dirty dog who observes for the Archies at Demirhisar?"

I have precisely the same hearty desire.

．　　　．　　　．　　　．　　　．

Later on Siebold changed over to scout machines. When he was through his course, he was sent to Jagdstaffel 38, which flew in the Vardar sector. There he went down in a fight with an English squadron, and his machine burst into flames when it crashed.

CHAPTER XIV

THE SLACKER

WE take off at 5 a.m. one morning. I am in the Rumpler two-seater with Wethekam, while Ahlen is flying the Halberstadt scout. Leaving the mountain mass of the Pinar Dagh on our left, we fly

a direct course for the Struma mouth. Ahlen cara-
coles lustily around us as his machine is considerably
faster than our two-seater. He flies ahead for a bit,
and then goes into a turn which brings him out
behind our tail—only to overhaul us quickly again.
As arranged, we reach the lines between Lake Takhino
and the sea at a height of 3,000 metres.

It is a wonderfully clear day—just made for photography. And the fact that the English Archies are
merciful enough to refrain from firing at us makes the
glorious morning all the more beautiful. In all
probability they are silent because they find difficulty
in sighting us against the sun.

As I mean to make vertical exposures to-day, I
signal Wethekam by a whack to fly straight over the
trenches. I start my photography, but much to my
annoyance I am forced to interrupt it after the first
snap because the side-wind has pushed us off the
objective. I signal to Wethekam to cut his engine,
so that he can understand my instructions.

" We must keep more——" I break off with a start,
because a shell has burst close below us. But I quickly
recover from the shock and complete my sentence :
" . . . more to the right ! "

Wethckam edges the machine gently to the
required direction, but the English do not seem pleased
about it. They send shell upon shell and shrapnel
upon shrapnel up to us. One snow-white cloud
follows another out of the blue morning air, and almost
at the same moment each detonation thunders into
our ears—a sign of close proximity. The Tommies
have worked out the range to a nicety, and their
shells burst exactly at our height. And now they
become still more unfriendly, for they put up a barrage
ahead of us, so that we have to sheer off and then
approach our objective anew. (Photograph 31.)

I use the involuntary period of leisure to look round for Ahlen. He is flying his circles high above us. As soon as we have come out of the turn the enemy has forced upon us and reached the right wing of the positions I whack Wethekam on to his course again.

And then—just a short distance above us—crack! We give vent to involuntary ducks—the usual reflex action of ground fighting which is not the slightest use to us up here in the air. I look up and to one side of me.

A thick black ball of smoke hurtles over our heads. I am amazed. Hitherto they have always plastered us with white shell-bursts—so why these black ones all of a sudden? When patrolling over the lines, one is always suspicious of novelties, because they seldom bring pleasant surprises.

I peer overboard in my excitement and soon discover the solution of the mystery. Two kilometres off the coast lies an English monitor, which is giving a little friendly assistance to the fire of the land battery.

" Oh the swine! Black smoke! "

I put Wethekam on to the objective for the third time. Bad photography to-day! But this time we also fail to get on to the mark; the detonations go off around us at the briefest intervals. Any practical work is out of the question.

I look round for our guardian angel as Wethekam approaches the objective for the fourth time. He has vanished!

My mood, which has been considerably troubled by the accurate shooting of the Archies, continues to deteriorate. I have a raging anger in my stomach. Probably Ahlen has found the potting so unpleasant that he has withdrawn to a safer distance.

But the next moment I feel ashamed of such sus-
picions. It would be inconceivable of him to abandon
us! But where has the fellow got to? Perhaps it is
just a chance that I cannot locate him, for up here one
has to depend mainly on one's eyes because the roar
of one's own engine makes it impossible for the ear to
catch the sound of any other machine.

Well, be that as it may—I shall carry on with the
job. It is a pity, however, that I must keep my own
eyes skinned for enemy aircraft. So once more into
the witches' cauldron!

Then a good idea strikes me. Once, when I was
flying in the west, the French Archies got me into a
nasty fix over Epernay. I simply dropped a thousand
metres; as they did not tumble to the trick, they kept
their fuse-lengths the same, so that the shells burst a
long way above our heads. Perhaps this ruse may
serve us to-day! And I shall get much better photos
if it does. I bend over to Wethekam's ear and display
two outspread fingers before his eyes.

" Down to two thousand! "

Wethekam nods, throttles down and goes into a
wide turn, which brings him back to the starting-point
for the objective. But we are only two thousand
metres up as we approach it.

And—lo and behold!—my trickery prospers to-day
as well. I finish the first series of exposures at my
ease, without hearing a single detonation. (Photograph 32.)

As we approach once more to photograph the
second strip I have another look round for Ahlen.
Not a sign of the wretched fellow. Then I whack
Wethekam's crash helmet and point upward.

He wriggles about on his seat with joy. The whole
of the straight line we have flown without a single

swerve is plastered with black and white shell bursts. But all of them, without exception, are a thousand metres too high.

Nevertheless, I have a heartfelt wish to get the second series done. Firstly, the Archie gunners down below must become aware of their folly in time and correct the length of their fuses. That would involve painful consequences for us at the low height at which we are flying.

Moreover a greater peril threatens us. We have been pottering about this region for a full hour, and it is quite inconceivable that the English airmen should have failed to take note of us. They are generally on the spot so quickly. Where are the fellows to-day? In any case, the password is: "Keep your eyes skinned!"

I look all round me. The air is still clear. Meanwhile we have reached the positions, and I can resume my photography. My luck holds good; as before, the shells are still a thousand metres too high.

So now I can run off a third series. I have another look for Ahlen during our approaching turn. He is and remains invisible.

The third strip is completed without disturbance. My luck seems almost too good. There is not even a jam when I change the plates. With a smile of happiness I stow the exposed plates in the rack and bend over to Wethekam.

"Finished!"

He gives me a nod of pleasure in the mirror and sheers off eastward. Homeward!

Despite my joy at the happy completion of my job, we cannot help a certain feeling of uneasiness. We cannot believe in such a large slice of good luck. It is to be hoped that Ahlen is all right.

.   .   .   .   .

"Is the one-seater back yet?" I ask the works master as soon as we have landed.

"No, not yet, sir."

After sending my plates to be developed by the photography section and forwarding my report to divisional H.Q., I wandered about the aerodrome uneasily with Wethekam, so that I could await Ahlen's landing or at least, a report concerning him from one of the observation posts at the front.

At last the drone of an engine became audible in the distance. If only it was his machine!

And it really was! As soon as the Halberstadt came to a standstill, his long legs strode towards us.

"Well, you've got a bad conscience, my friend," I growled to myself. "I'm curious to know what your excuse will be."

Meanwhile Ahlen arrived. He beamed with joy as he stood before me. I assumed a threatening attitude, but it was only half so serious as it seemed, for I was heartily glad to see him and his machine safe and sound on the aerodrome again.

"Well, you old joyrider! What have you been doing with yourself all this time?"

Ahlen did not appear to notice my serious undertone, for he continued to beam.

"I landed at Radulevo!"

"Forced landing?"

"No, voluntary!"

Then I had to show my displeasure. "Well, I never—instead of protecting us!"

But then Ahlen could keep his secret no longer. "But I did, sir. I went there in the course of my job. I shot down the Sopwith two-seater that wanted to attack you, sir." (See sketch at chapter heading.)

"It is——"

Impossible to let him go on speaking. I shook his hand in fervent appreciation of the pleasure I shared with him. "Splendid! Heartiest congratulations!"

Ahlen laughed.

"I attacked him in a turn as soon as I saw him making for you from Lake Takhino, sir. He didn't spot me because I was higher than he, and so I got a good burst on to him at once. Then we had a long bout of turns; I let off four hundred shots before I smashed his engine. He's down close to Radulevo. I landed close to him immediately afterwards." (Photograph 33.)

He extracted a piece of paper from his pocket.

"Sopwith two-seater, Type L. Cl. T., No. 5,108, with 110 h.p. Clerget rotary engine, Type 9 B., No. 372. Pilot, Lieutenant Bernard Brady, severely wounded; observer, Lieutenant Leslie Marsh, slightly wounded. Both of the R.N.A.S. Vrasta aerodrome."

Once more I shook Ahlen's hand. "Heartiest congratulations for the first credited victory and best thanks for the good comradeship!"

I raised my eyebrows as I turned to Wethekam.

"So much good luck is enough to kill you. I never saw a sign of the English machine."

"Nor did I!" said Wethekam in a whisper.

CHAPTER XV

OUR AERODROME ON FIRE

I SUMMONED all the squads to the aerodrome.
"You have heard that the English set the corn-
fields in the Sarishaban plain on fire with their bombs.

We are going to spoil their fun if they try the same game on with our aerodrome. I want a shallow ditch dug round each tent—at least three metres wide. All other work suspended for the present. The Bulgarians will cut the grass for us as well."

.   .   .   .   .

A few days later I was sitting in the photographic section's office, calculating the value of the snaps taken on my last flight. Suddenly the telephone buzzed. A minute later, Angeloff stood before my table.

" Squadron of seven English machines, from direction of Badimal, flew over Angista station. Heading for Drama ! "

As they had not dropped their bombs on Angista, the visit was evidently intended for us.

" Anyone warned the aerodrome ? " I asked.

Angeloff nodded. Picking up my glasses, I stepped to the doorway. I heard the rattle of Eschwege's engine on the aerodrome and saw white shell-bursts in the air, somewhere over Angista. But then Eschwege suddenly cut his engine.

What could that mean ? Something gone wrong with his machine ! What a pity he could not take off in time !

The minutes dragged out endlessly. Now I could already hear the iron song of the English machines droning above us ; soon afterwards I saw the seven machines as black streaks floating in the leaden grey sky. A slight touch of fear crept over me. I could only hope that Eschwege might get his machine going before the first bombs burst.

I put my glasses to my eyes again and directed them on to the aerodrome. Thank Heaven—Eschwege was climbing back into his machine—his mechanic was swinging the propeller—and now his engine had caught on.

High time, too, for in a few seconds the first bombs were bound to explode. At last, at last the Albatros began to move slowly, and at the same moment three mighty cascades of soil rose up. Luckily the bombs were badly aimed, for they fell on the neighbouring fields.

And now the Albatros left the ground. A hundred-weight load was lifted from my heart, for a few seconds later more explosive bombs came down—right in the middle of the aerodrome this time. I searched for the machine squad with my glasses. The men had already vanished into their dug-out.

So now I was able to watch the further proceedings calmly. The English dropped twenty-five bombs; then they all went into wide turns and flew back to the front. There were four bombers, flying side by side, in good order, while above them cruised an escort of three scouts. Meanwhile I had lost sight of Eschwege.

So I turned my glasses on to the aerodrome again while waiting for my car. I smiled mirthfully. Five, at least, of the twenty-five bombs were bound to be duds, for over the spots where they fell hovered thin clouds of smoke and dust, which the wind was gradually dispersing. And now I could see through them—but what was that?

At three spots thick white clouds were rising through the thinning mist. The aerodrome was on fire! The wall of flame was pushing swiftly on towards the tents.

A second later I sat in my car, whirling out to the aerodrome. From afar I could see my brave fellows running about the ground. When I arrived after some anxious minutes, our united forces contrived to extinguish the fire in the neighbourhood of the tents.   On the far side, where there were no erections, it continued to eat its way through the dry grass.

I breathed freely.   Yes, I could trust my lads. When the last bomb fell, they opposed the oncoming blaze with hand-extinguishers.   It was no easy job for them, because the dry grass burnt like tinder and allowed the flames a fairly quick progress.   By making a detour we were just in time to assail the fire on its flanks.   It was also a bit of luck that the extinguishers worked.   All of them emitted such powerful jets at once that we managed to master the flames with them. (See sketch at chapter heading.)

Now we had only to beat out the glowing patches with spades and crowbars.   It was well for us that Lieutenant-Colonel Asmanoff had sent his squad of Bulgarian mowers.   If the grass had still retained its long stalks, we should hardly have succeeded in checking the fire.

In reality the five " duds " were therefore incendiary bombs.   The explosive bombs were only dropped in order to hinder us in the work of extinguishing the flames.   Glad as I was at the absence of any material damage, my joy in this respect was trifling compared with the feeling of happiness I experienced when I saw that Eschwege had taken off untouched by any of the falling bombs.

.   .   .   .   .

Barely an hour later, we heard the song of an engine. Eschwege was returning.   He landed a few minutes afterwards.

" Nothing doing ! " he grumbled.   " The English-men kept a perfect squadron order.   I exchanged shots with them all the way from Angista to the lines, and I'm sure I put some hits into several of their machines, but I did not manage to shoot any down. As soon as ever I got a burst on to one of them, two or three others always tackled me ! "

Meanwhile his mechanics had examined the machine.

" A bullet through the right upper wing," announced one of them.

He waved it aside with a contemptuous gesture. " There is plenty of room there ! "

CHAPTER XVI

IN THE EXPLOSION

AFTER a short spell of cooler weather the oppres-
sive sultriness weighed down upon the plain
once more. After our meal we sat on the veranda in

the pleasant cool of the evening, doing nothing in particular. Naturally, Eschwege's thoughts were centred only on flying.

" The Thasos brethren will soon be laying their hot eggs again, now that everything's dried up," he suggested.

I nodded my concurrence. " Of course ! Even though you've polished off six out of their twenty during the last half year—they are Englishmen ! If you shoot down nineteen of them, number twenty will still make an effort to do something. I'd try waiting for them at Iralti again, if I were you ! "

Eschwege considered the point.

" I'd prefer to leave them in peace for the present," he said, " so that they can get accustomed again to taking things easy in the air. One mustn't make life too hard for them ; otherwise they'll come across at such a huge height that I can't possibly reach them from my forward landing-ground. Meanwhile, I propose to lie in wait for their pals from Orljak."

.   .   .   .   .

All was quiet on the Struma front, however. The English machines were certainly in the air every day, but unfortunately—or rather, fortunately for them—they never flew in the same part of the sky as Eschwege. After three days he was fed up and so returned to Iralti. I grew anxious when he was not back by the end of the afternoon, but in the evening he arrived—as hungry as a wolf and parched with thirst.

" Rotten ! " he growled. " I hung about all day in that swinish heat and couldn't see a single tail ! "

" Yes, you had bad luck to-day ! Two land machines from the Struma front flew quite low over Porna station and dropped their bombs."

" Oh ?   Then I'd better try the Struma front again
to-morrow ! "

And so it came to pass, but unfortunately, there
was clear air there, while quite a lively lot of traffic
issued from Thasos.   A squadron of eight machines
came to trouble the Sarishaban plain, where they
caused three fires.   Eschwege was furious.

" It's a swinish business.   Our Staffel has a hundred
and sixty kilometres of front ; wherever one is, the
enemy is somewhere else ! "

.   .   .   .   .

The following morning he flew off to Iralti again.

I heard his machine when sitting in my office in the
midday hours.   The joyful certainty flashed into my
mind—he had got another !   When I rang up the aerodrome, I received news that he was on his way to me,
and almost the next moment I heard him calling out.
He fell on my neck as I emerged from the office.

" Come to report most obediently—got another ! "

I wrung his hand joyfully and gazed in astonishment
at the eyes which gleamed with a strange brightness
from a face black with soot.

" Well, who's made you up so beautifully ? "

He whistled through his teeth.

" I nearly gave myself a coat of paint.   As a matter
of fact, I ran into an explosion.   I'd been waiting
out there since sunrise, and—just imagine their cheek
—they came across at the very same time as before;
11.30 a.m. sharp !

" There were four of them this trip.   All Sopwith
two-seaters—fast land machines.   To-day, however,
I didn't let them drop their bombs first, but took off
the moment I saw them, for I had no desire to experience those ghastly minutes again—when the
English sailed peacefully homeward over my head

with me down below, unable to get my engine going. Also I knew that after their previous experience they'd be keeping a sharp look-out for me.

"So I took off as soon as I saw them with the naked eye. They spotted me at once, got rid of their bombs in open country and made a right-about turn. But they kept together beautifully—I take off my hat to them for that! As soon as ever I attacked one, the other three promptly closed up and worried me with their machine-guns. The threads of their tracer bullets were almost shaving my nose as they streaked past—pretty uncomfortable it was!"

"But you pulled it off all the same?"

"Coming to that in a moment. I had to break away and turn four or five times, but kept on attacking. Each time I had to sheer off to dodge a burst. We flew across the coast and were making for Thasos, shooting and turning all the time.

"Then I lost my wool. I picked out the one that was flying deepest and went for him in a nose-dive. The other three promptly carried out their part of the programme and spun a net of tracers round me.

"My victim saw that it was a matter of life and death for him, and put his stick hard down for a desperate dash. But this time I refused to let go, and so approached quite close, shooting all the time. Just as I was about to go into a turn, I saw a jet of flame spurt out from his cockpit, and the next moment the Sopwith burst up with a bang. I promptly pulled my machine up, but for a few seconds I was swallowed up in the haze and smoke. At the same time I got a smack from below by a gust, which was worse than anything I've experienced in a thunderstorm. I couldn't hear or see a thing!" (See sketch at chapter heading.)

He spat on the ground. " I've still got such a wicked taste in my mouth ! But it doesn't worry me, for I scored a victory ! "

" And the other three ? "

" Did a quick bolt. I wanted to get another— then my engine suddenly began to sputter. The rev-counter dropped back to 800, picked up again and then jumped backwards and forwards most woefully.

" I got a hell of a fright, for I had dropped down to 400 metres in the course of the fight. If my engine gave out, I was for it, just like those two Englishmen I forced down on to the water that time. So I turned back at once—and found myself at least five kilometres from the mainland coast. So I couldn't reach dry land in a glide. And then—my heart stood still—the hand slid back to zero, and the next moment my engine went dead ! "

" Then it was hit in the fight ? "

" No, no ! I examined it before I came along— everything O.K. But it probably swallowed a dose of burnt-out gas when I barged into the cloud of that explosion and felt dreadfully sick. Anyhow, I saw I must do something quickly if I loved life. I had to put everything on one card. If I was lucky, I could get the propeller going again by putting the machine into a vertical dive—and then—if my luck held—the engine might pick up again. So off I went ! I put the stick down hard and whizzed off towards the waves on my head !

" And then—barely thirty metres above the sea— the force of the air-pressure set the propeller going again—a lovely shiver went through the machine— the engine had started again !

" I eased off gradually. The rev-counter moved forward slowly until it was wobbling round 1,600 again."

I breathed a sigh of relief. " Thank heaven for that ! And what did you think about when you were tumbling down ? "

He laughed.

" Well, the usual things first. Seemed surprised that the machine suddenly stopped when it had been going all right. Thought someone must have been doing something to it. And then I hoped the observation post on the shore had seen the Englishman burst up. I wanted you to know in any case that I had settled the fellow ! "

CHAPTER XVII

A NOISY FAREWELL PARTY

MY face grew longer and longer as the Greek summer progressed. One after another of my people broke down under the effect of the murderous Greek climate.

Lieutenant von Wobeser started the business with

a violent attack of fever. After being down on his back for several weeks he was so debilitated that I was forced to put him in for a transfer to lighter duty.

He was followed by Acting Officer von der Weppen, in whom some typhus bacilli took considerable interest. As Dr. Woermann made a correct diagnosis, he was sent off to hospital in time and nursed through his illness.

Unfortunately, our medicine man took more care of his friends than himself. A gastric fever assailed him so violently that he had to beat a retreat. Dr. Frenzl became our " plaster box " in his stead.

Likewise, I had to push off Kuhlo and Stattaus, because their stomachs and intestines refused to carry on.

Even Eschwege went very limp for a few days. When I gave him a searching look, he protested energetically : " What ! Me ill ? Impossible ! I've no time to be ill when there are so many Englishmen knocking around ! "

His was, indeed, no mere heroic gesture. After a couple of days off he was able to fly again, and on the third day he shot down his fifteenth victim.

．　．　．　．　．

The worst ravages were the work of the malaria.

What was the use of sleeping under nets with fine meshes every night and putting gauze blinds in front of every window and door ! The tiny, nimble mosquitoes still found their way to our blood. Naturally we obtained no replacements for the smitten, because the whole of the Balkans were down with fever.

We should have found it a heavy burden to bear, but for one consolation : the Tommies on the other side of the lines were getting it even worse. I quote from an English account :

> "When we went to Macedonia, we knew it was a fever country. But no one was able to realize the full extent of the deadliness of—for example—the Struma plain. Our people sank under the malaria like grass-blades under a scythe. One infantry battalion dwindled from its strength of 1,000 to one officer and nineteen men."

And for a time, only two of the twenty aircraft crews on Thasos aerodrome were fit for duty.

. . . . .

I felt very seedy one morning when I had received a summons to Divisional H.Q. Nevertheless, I took my stick and crawled through the sweltering streets. I did not get far, because my feet refused duty, so that I had to sit down on some stone steps, completely exhausted. Then I struggled back home wearily and flopped down on my bed. Our doctor felt my pulse and took my temperature.

Malaria tropica !

I have not many memories of the subsequent thirty-six hours. I only know that an indescribable longing for cool and shade tortured the fantasies of my fever.

I tried to get up again on the morning of the third day. I succeeded and soon learnt the use of my feet again, even though unable to dispense with my stick for a while. My attempt to fly again was punished with spasmodic stomach attacks. But at least, I managed to carry on the business of the Staffel.

Several days later I received a telephone message from Captain von Blomberg, our O.C. Aviation :

> "Four weeks sick leave. Afterwards you are

in command of the Staff Photography Section until complete recovery."

Much as I loathed the idea of parting from my beloved Staffel, I did not like to refuse this post, which was a preliminary to the appointment on the General Staff I desired. It was arranged that I should report at Uskub a week later and then go on leave. So I had ample time to initiate Lieutenant König into the business. He had already understudied me on several occasions.

.   .   .   .   .

The evening before I flew away there was a large farewell party, to which we invited the other Germans working in Drama. The farewell oration was delivered by Eschwege, who concluded with the words :

" I am only sorry that I cannot bring down an Englishman to-day in his honour ! Well, perhaps one may come along—morning is still a long way off ! "

We cheered him for that, but we were soon destined to forgo our laughter. Half an hour later the telephone buzzed.

" A machine took off from Thasos."

Eschwege beamed.

" Just what I said ! I hope he'll come here instead of visiting the sea-fliers ! "

The latter, however, appeared to be his destination, for a further report soon came in :

" English aircraft heading for Xanthi."

Eschwege pulled a wry face. " What a pity ! Well, it can't be helped ! Then we'll just put another glass or so inside us ! "

This proposal found favour. Our merry mood

rose—until it was burst a quarter of an hour later. It was then 11.10 p.m.

"Crrrackk ! ! ! Crrrrackk ! ! ! "

Two further heavy cracks followed. Eschwege was depressed.

"That spoils the fun ! If only I had taken off ! "

I hung on to the telephone. A report came through from the aerodrome. "Heavy bomb fell close to the one-seaters' tent. Halberstadts damaged by air pressure."

Our merry mood was over. We wandered out to the aerodrome.

Eschwege's beautiful machine ! The woodwork was splintered and the canvas of the cockpit's walling hung in shreds. But a closer investigation showed that although several framework parts were damaged, the engine and main spars remained unscathed.

"A bad leave-taking for me," I said to Eschwege. "And so I'll pay my farewell visit to the Thasos brethren in your company and drop a few bombs down on them. Perhaps we'll thus get them out of the habit of these immoral night trips."

Eschwege was all fire and flames for it. But König held me back. "You're still too shaky from your malaria ! Please leave it to me ! "

"All right ! " It was not long before I had his Rumpler out and ready to start. While the armoury master saw to the machine-gun, the bombs were stowed on board—four explosive bombs in the rack and two incendiary bombs in the cockpit. Everything was ready about midnight.

"You'll have good visibility in the moonlight. So Hals und Beinbruch ! "

Eschwege crept into the pilot's seat and ran his engine. The exhaust gases spat themselves out in a red jet of flame. Eschwege nodded, and König climbed in. A brief waving of hands—the big bird began to move slowly—her pace increased—a wee hop—then she lifted herself from the ground and winged her steady way out into the moonlight night. ...

. . . . .

"What are we going to do meanwhile?" asked Lakemann, the civil servant, who was always thirsty.

"We'll wait here till they come back!"

As I arranged to have our "bowl" brought out there for sociability's sake, he agreed.

Our conversation turned exclusively on the two comrades who had taken off and the process of bombing. As a matter of fact, it was really a miracle that the English had done so little harm in all their numerous attacks on our aerodrome. The machine which they had damaged that night could soon be repaired, so that the only total loss we had to book during my time was the reserve scout, which had been burnt when a direct hit fell on its tent. Thanks to the thrustful activity of Eschwege, we had been still luckier in the air, winning sixteen victories without losing a single machine, while the only severely wounded casualty was our dear Eckardt.

Gradually the conversation died down. All the more fervently our thoughts circled round the two friends in the air. Again and again we turned our glances to the mountains of Philippi, behind which lay the island of Thasos.

And then—to south-eastward the sky flamed up in a vivid red, which gradually assumed a deeper hue. I looked at my watch: 1 a.m.

The suspense grew intolerable. For a moment an icy shiver ran through my limbs. Had our comrades been shot down in flames? But I quickly shook off this horrible thought. My belief in our luck was too strong. Moreover, one small machine could not set half the sky aglow. No, there was only one magnificent possibility—that König had aimed truly and well!

The telephone's bell rang as I hastened to the tent which contained the instrument. And a few instants later our faithful Angeloff came out and announced in trembling accents the report from the Bulgarian observation post in the neighbourhood of Kavala:

" Thasos aerodrome on fire!"

It was impossible to express the outburst of our exultant joy in words. When the reflection of mighty explosions quivered in the sky a few minutes later and we realized that the bomb sheds were going up in the air, I had to turn away to hide the tears in my eyes.

. . . . . .

What had happened?

Eschwege and König head seawards as soon as they have taken off. After a half-hour's flight they can make out Thasos ahead of them. When a searchlight flares up and begins to scour the air, König shuts it up with a few shots. Then the quickfirer grows lively and sends its gleaming phosphorus shells aloft. Luckily, its aim is directed to another quarter of the sky.

König bends overboard to take a look at his target. The huge gleaming Bessoneau hangars at the edge of a mulberry plantation flank the aerodrome in a wide semi-circle and look near enough to touch.

" Ruck! ruck! ruck! ruck!"

The four explosive bombs whirl into the depths.

Ten seconds later the hits flash up. They lie very close to a hangar.

There are still the two incendiary bombs to go. That means another approach to the objective. Once more the inquisitive searchlight and its machine-gun must be warned to keep quiet. König selects a hangar and gives Eschwege a light tap on his left shoulder. That means : " We are going over too far right ! "

Eschwege puts the Rumpler slowly round to the left. Holding the two live incendiary bombs under his arm, König peers down below. Now for it ! He drops them with a second's interval.

Into a turn again to watch the bursts. He strains his eyes to search the ground. But he sees no burst. The incendiary bombs must have touched ground some time ago. Are they duds ?

" Home ! "

Eschwege nods and makes for the mainland beyond the sea. Suddenly they both start in amazement. A red glow is mirrored on their wings. A swift glance behind gives a welcome explanation—a hangar containing six machines blazes up to heaven like a huge torch. The incendiary bombs have fired it !

Eschwege promptly puts the machine into a turn. Back ! As soon as they reach the aerodrome, they drop down to get a close view of the fireworks. The hangar is past saving now. Moreover, the grass— dry as hay—has taken fire. The English soldiers are trying to extinguish the blaze on the aerodrome.

That, of course, they must not do ! Eschwege puts his machine on her nose, and fires as he whirls down towards the aerodrome. Then he circles round the scene of the conflagration so that König can rake it with his pivotable gun. The English reatret under the hail of bullets ; the fire spreads outwards until at last it reaches the mulberry planta- tion.   Now they can go home at ease ; the furnaces are well stoked.   (See sketch at chapter heading.)

König perches himself the wrong way round on his tip-up seat and stares at the burning aerodrome. And then—a mighty explosion hurls sheaves of fire up into the sky ; the flames have reached the bomb depot and sent its contents up.

Once more Eschwege goes into a prolonged turn, so that he too may enjoy the spectacle.   Then, at last, he puts the machine on her course for Drama.   Petrol is running low.

Further explosions follow.

The score is paid !

.   .   .   .   .

Meanwhile, we still sat waiting on the aerodrome. It was nearly two o'clock.   Where were our couple ?

They had been up for almost two hours.   Their purpose was achieved ; the blood-red sky and the observation post had given us news on that point. Then " rrrrrt ! " the telephone announced another message.

" Two enemy aircraft making for Drama from Kavala ! "

We started at one another in amazement.   Retribu- tion for our retribution ?   Well, just what we might expect from those dashing Englishmen !

But where was our machine ?   It was to be hoped that it would not return at some stupid moment when it would be forced to land in the midst of the English bombs.   We sat there, waiting in anxious suspense.

And then the drone of an engine sounded in our ears.   But by the sound that could only be our

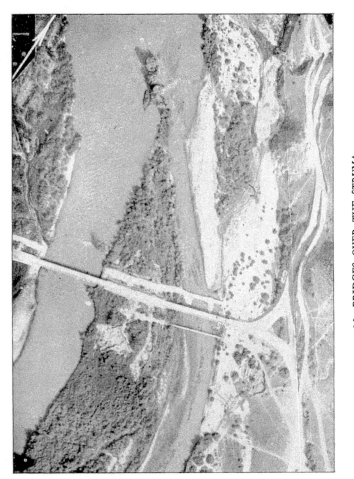

32. BRIDGES OVER THE STRUMA

33. AHLEN'S VICTIM

people. I hoped they arrived before the English came along. I did not need to put out any flares because Eschwege always managed his nocturnal landings without illumination.

We stared until our eyes were starting from our heads. And then—at last, we knew it was our Rumpler! It came down to the aerodrome in a beautiful glide.

Now we could see its black shadow hovering over the ground in the moonlight. It dropped nearer and nearer to the earth, which swallowed it up as it landed. It came to a stop after a short run, and then it taxied off to its tent in a wide sweep. We hastened thither to offer our comrades heartfelt congratulations on their success.

" But get out quickly now! Two English machines have been reported! "

" Who knows whether they're coming here? "

The doubt appeared to be well founded, for we could hear nothing more of them. And then the telephone rang again.

" There's only one machine! And it has flown to Drama! "

Then we laughed, for it was plain to us that they must have heard our own machine. The Bulgarians had mistaken its echo in the mountains for a second machine.

We remained on the aerodrome until 2.30 a.m., staring across in the direction of Thasos. The sky was still blood-red, and the red fingers of explosions still groped up towards the stars.

We could feel satisfied. It was really a roaring success.

.   .   .   .   .

On the following morning I sent König and

M

Corporal Keller to Thasos, with Eschwege as an escort, so that they could photograph the scene of the conflagration.

The English were not so artful as we had been on a similar occasion. They had put up no new tents over the " dark point." Probably they had no spare ones. But in any case the blackened grass and the crater made by our bursting bombs were clear evidence of the success of our nocturnal raid. (Photographs 34 and 35.)

And so we could feel more satisfied with our photographs than the Tommies whom we had deceived so meanly on that former occasion.

CHAPTER XVIII

A BALLOON AND A HALF

ON September 23rd I took command of the Staff Photography Section. I still remained in close touch with my old Staffel, because the daily reports

M*

and aerial photographs from all flying units on the Salonica front passed through my hands.

Ten days later—on October 3rd—came the first tidings of victory :

"Lieutenant von Eschwege shot down B.E. English one-seater in flames, west of Sarmusaki. Wreckage between lines in our patrol area."

His sixteenth ! And it was not long before he made himself conspicuous again :

"Scout attacked English motor-boat on west shore, Lake Takhino, from 1,000 metres. Put burst of 300 shots into boat."

That was the boat in which the English had proposed to visit us !

.   .   .   .   .

About this time the captive balloon belonging to Balloon Section 17 popped up in the neighbourhood of Orljak on the Struma front after a fairly long interval.

Ever since its reappearance, Eschwege went about with a thoughtful face. But he invariably shook his head when anyone remarked :

"New captive balloon up ! What about it, Eschwege ? "

"Captive balloon, eh ? No, not in my line ! "

But on the morning of October 28th he secretly filled a belt with incendiary bullets and took off. For news had just come in from the front that the balloon had been sent up to a height of 800 metres. He decided to take a chance at it.

He considered the point ; this was another case for a surprise attack. If the English spotted him too soon, their Archies would put up a barrage, and send their scouts up to protect it. And—worse still—they would haul the balloon down. So trickery was the only way !

When he took off, he headed for the mountains, from the cover of which he planned to make a dash for the lines with the sun at his back.

A quarter of an hour later he has gained the right distance. Yonder, far below him, the balloon sways in the morning breeze.

Eschwege throttles well down in order to avoid an untimely betrayal of his presence by the sound of his engine. Then he swoops down on the balloon in a prolonged glide.

He has not yet been seen. The observer is leaning out of his basket-work car, scanning the Bulgarian positions through his glasses. The enemy's Archie battery has also failed to notice his arrival.

When he is only 600 metres away, he bends over and gets the huge envelope into his sights. His aim does not need to be so deadly accurate as in an air-fight—as long as he keeps roughly on the mark, he can hit this haystack of a target.

Now he is within 300 metres—a pressure on the trigger-button—and " tackackackackack ! " the two machine guns rattle away. The threads of smoke vanish into the envelope—the balloon must break out in flames in a moment.

He approaches within ten metres of it, firing all the time—he pulls the stick on to his chest—and just clears the mass. Then follows a steep turn.

A bitter disappointment : the balloon is not on fire.

The gunners below are running to their guns. And the balloon's observer, wearing his parachute, climbs on to the edge of the car to jump out. He is still hesitating.   Probably he is a novice, making his first jump.

Again Eschwege attacks !   He fires from both guns.   A backward glance.   The balloon is not yet on fire !

A bad business !

The English observer evidently thinks the same. His situation has become painful, and he jumps. Eschwege sees him swaying down earthward under the white parachute.

A third attack !   But still no ignition !

The machine-guns cackle up to him from the ground.   Some shells burst threateningly near.   What does he care !   That gas-bag must go down !

A fourth approach.   The guns cease fire for fear of damaging the balloon.

" Tackackackackackackackack ! "

Once more the little clouds of smoke disappear into the silver-grey envelope.   And then—at last !—a tiny red flame quivers out and grows apace.   The balloon is on fire !   (See sketch at chapter heading.)

The missiles of the artillery and machine-guns howl upward again.   Eschwege worms his way through them in irregular turns.

Some shrapnels are still singing behind him.   Too short !

Victory !

.   .   .   .   .

Several days later there is a new balloon up in place of the one he shot down.   On November 9th, Eschwege rings up the front.

" How high ? "

" Only 250 metres, because of thick clouds."

Eschwege deliberates.

"It's got to go down," he decides.

He sneaks up to its vicinity above the clouds and makes a dive at it through a hole in them. Then— the left gun jams. Anxious hopes—if only the other gun will carry on! But after thirty rounds it lets him down.

Eschwege circles round the balloon twice in the fire the Archies have hastily started, tugging at his guns. Surely he can get one, at least, of them to see reason? In vain!

The observer gets nervous. He jumps down. But to-day he is not so lucky as on the previous occasion. The parachute fails to open. His body plunges earthwards at an ever-increasing speed. And when the parachute opens at last, it is too late. The speed is too great—the straps tear away—and the Englishman's body crashes to the ground.

Eschwege is still circling round the balloon and banging at his guns. The fire from the machine-guns and artillery pieces becomes increasingly unpleasant. Already there are several gaping holes in his wings.

The jams cannot be cleared. So there is nothing left for him but to retreat, however bitter this decision may be for him.

And this time, too, he succeeds in emerging from the enemy's fire unscathed. He crosses the English trenches at a bare 100 metres.

His face is white with disappointment.

CHAPTER XIX

THE KING OF THE AIR

THE two-seaters of the Staffel raided Lahana
ae odrome in squadron formation on November
12th.   When they landed, König spoke to Eschwege.
"Better leave the balloon alone for the present!
The English have planted a crowd of guns by it.

And they hauled it down and put up a hefty barrage as soon as we approached."

Eschwege laughed.

" So easy for you to say ' leave it alone,' my dear fellow.   I wanted to leave that balloon alone, but it won't leave me alone ! "

.   .   .   .   .

On November 15th Eschwege rang up the front to inquire whether the balloon was up again.

" Yes, but you can't attack it to-day ! Firstly it's only 500 metres up, and secondly there are three English machines cruising about over Orljak to protect it."

Eschwege was wrapped in thought as he walked across the aerodrome.

" And thirdly, I'll have it down all the same," he vowed.

His mechanic came to him when he was in his tent.

" What ammunition are you taking up to-day, sir?"

Eschwege reflected.

" In any case, you'd better put me some incendiary bullets in the right belt.   I don't know whether I can get a shot at it to-day.   But I'll be wild if I can and yet can't."

.   .   .   .   .

He takes off a quarter of an hour later.   Rain clouds hang over the Struma plain.   Not a single English machine is to be seen over the lines, but several of them are flying round the balloon in narrow circles.

Then the fever of battle takes possession of Eschwege.   By making skilful use of the clouds, he succeeds in approaching the balloon unseen.

On reaching the right distance, he puts his machine

down and swoops on the balloon in a vertical dive—
right between the machines of its astounded protectors.

It is a mad piece of audacity which can only meet
with success if he sets fire to the balloon at the first
onslaught. The English airmen will allow him no
time for a second attempt. And luck is with him
once more. The red flame dances on the envelope
after his first few shots. A turn—back to the front.

To left and right of him, above him and below, in
front and behind him shell and shrapnel are bursting.
But Eschwege slides back across the English lines
untouched.

The airmen give chase—but fly away cowed when
he turns back. With a joyful eye he watches the
burning envelope sink slowly earthwards.

His eighteenth confirmed victory !

.   .   .   .   .

The next few days brought thick clouds, but on
November 19th the weather cleared up somewhat.

A report from the front : " New balloon up over
Orljak ! "

.   .   .   .   .

König took hold of Eschwege's arm as he watched
his machine being pushed out of its tent.

" You don't mean to have another go at——"

Eschwege set his mind at rest with a gesture of denial.

" No, not to-day. I only want to have a look at
the fellows. Besides, there are so many airmen flying
about the place to protect it. Perhaps I can pick off
one of them."

He sees anti-aircraft fire over by Seres when about
to cross the lines half an hour later. He makes for it.

Two smears loom out of the air. A B.E. two-seater
and a Sopwith scout. He looks down. He is over

Kalendra, i.e., still on his own side of the lines.

He gets a burst on to the larger machine at his first onslaught. But meanwhile the scout hangs on behind him, so that he is flying in a cross fire. The B.E.'s observer is peppering him in front, and the Sopwith pilot from behind.

Doesn't matter!—He is so confident of victory to-day and feels so sure of his own invulnerability that he fastens on to the B.E.'s neck and refuses to budge.

And then—a cloud of smoke and a little flame that grows apace. . . .

Settled him!

The Sopwith bolts for the lines in a nose-dive when Eschwege throws his machine round in a sharp turn. What a pity! (See sketch at chapter heading.)

So he has time to see what the B.E. is doing. It is going down to earth in the form of a huge torch.

. . . . .

Eschwege found bad news awaiting him when he landed in Drama. Sergeant van Ahlen was not so lucky in his air-fight; he had been forced to land near Porna with a severe leg wound.

. . . . .

Eschwege takes off again in the afternoon. As if by some magic power, he is drawn once more to Orljak. The Bulgarian observations are correct. A new captive balloon is up. He notes with grim satisfaction that the English haul it down at lightning speed as soon as he approaches. Four protecting machines are circling round the air in which it floats.

A mad idea comes into his brain: "I'll see if you have any spunk!"

He puts his machine on to its nose and dives !

But the English are so discour.iged by his last victory that all four—here, so many kilometres behind their own lines, protected by their own artillery and machine guns—fly before the onslaught of a solitary German.

Eschwege laughs as he flies homeward.

He has earned the honourable title which the Bulgarians have bestowed on him.

Bjelomorrsko orel !

The Eagle of the Aegean Sea !

Now he is a veritable king of the air !

CHAPTER XX

THE LAST VICTORY

THE morning of November 21st dawned grey.
Eschwege filled both belts of his machine-gun
with incendiary bullets and was interspersing the
cartridges by the light of his experience. The
machine's two startled attendants wheeled it out.

Was he really going to attack the Orljak balloon again to-day ? At last Lance-Corporal Leonhardt plucked up courage.

" Wouldn't you do well to wait a bit before attacking the balloon, sir ? It would be your fourth attack on it within three weeks ! "

Eschwege laughed as he clapped him on the shoulder.

" My good man, I'm just in luck's way. And you never win anything if you don't take a risk ! "

Five minutes later he took off on the flight that was to be his last.

.   .   .   .   .

The lieutenant of the Bulgarian observation post, in the mountains to the north-west of Seres, was spooning up his morning soup when a Voynik entered his dug-out :

" Balona katschwa ! " (The balloon is going up !)

The officer stepped outside and looked through his telescope. He had to keep on screwing it up because the balloon disappeared from his field of vision again and again. It was still rising.

The officer followed its progress in amazement. This meant something special ! After Eschwege had shot down two of its fellows a week ago, the enemy aeronauts had grown very cautious, refusing to send their new envelopes up more than a few hundred metres.

So why was this one climbing so high to-day ? Had the English something particular to do ? Were they wanting to find out something ? Was it going to spot for a long-range gun ? Were they afraid of a Bulgarian attack ?

The Bulgarian observer got the balloon into his

threads again. Ah, now it had stopped rising!
It was swaying to and fro in wide oscillations, rocked
by the breeze of the youthful morning. The officer
turned to his assistant.

" Very high to-day ! "

" Eight hundred metres, at least. And there's an
observer in it again to-day. When Eschwege set the
second one on fire, the basket was empty ! "

The officer looked through the glass again. The
man was right ; he could see the English observer in
it quite plainly.

" I'm sure they're up to something ! "

The soldier shrugged his shoulders.

" Mosche-bi ! " (Perhaps !)

Then he raised his index finger and listened. His
ears caught a distant hum in the air.

" The English airmen are coming up now to protect
the balloon against Eschwege ! "

The officer also listened excitedly. But then he
laughed.

" Tschuj szamo (But can't you hear) ; that's not an
English engine. It's a German one, it's Eschwege !
A good thing he's on the spot before the airmen over
there have had their sleep out ! "

The soldier fetched a pair of field-glasses from the
dug-out and searched the sky. His officer was right
—it was Eschwege ! The tiny machine was now in
his glasses ; it was heading for Orljak from a great
height over the mountains. So Eschwege wanted to
attack the balloon a fourth time ! In an excited voice
the soldier called his comrades to come and be
witnesses of the next victory.

And now the drone of the engine died away. The
slender bird lowered her beak and swooped. All were
breathless with excitement.

The officer stared through the telescope. Oh, how splendid! The English had not noticed Eschwege yet. Last time they put up a heavy barrage in front of the balloon while its assailant was still some kilometres away, but to-day, on the contrary, not one cloudlet had gone up from their guns. The balloon's observer also looked quite carefree as he leant over the edge of his basket.

This balloon was also bound to go down in flames unless Eschwege's guns jammed. The next few seconds would decide the issue! The Bulgarians stood in expectant silence. But the English artillery had not fired a shot yet!

The officer stared feverishly through the glass. Now the German machine dived into his field of vision—now he was swooping on his prey like an eagle—now he must be shooting. Had his incendiary bullets set it on fire? They would soon see!

Now he was within a few metres of the balloon— now the machine raised its head ahead—now it flitted over the balloon with a bare margin of space— and now the envelope was taking fire.

Hurrah!

But there was something different this time; the balloon had not started its blaze with a tiny flame as on previous occasions—to-day it flared up all at once to a mighty pillar of fire. Burning shreds from the envelope writhed slowly earthwards.

The overpowering suspense of the Bulgarian soldiers eased itself off in a tempestuous shout of exultation. Only the officer felt a dread foreboding which made his heart tremble.

Where was Eschwege? Had his lucky star guided him safely through the terrific explosion again, just as it did that time over the sea by Thasos?

34. BEFORE

AND AFTER

35. OUR BOMBING RAID ON THASOS

36. R.F.C. OFFICERS CARRYING ESCHWEGE'S COFFIN

Yes—thank Heaven—he was preserved. For now he plainly saw the machine emerge from the smoke and sheer away. (See sketch at chapter heading.)

But—oh horror !—it was going down over the left wing—now it was in a sideslip—and then, impelled by its heavy engine, it went down on to its nose and whirled earthwards. It was terrible ! It was impossible to realize that Eschwege was no longer alive !

The officer turned to his men in anxious fear. But they had only seen the balloon go down, and laughed as they hugged one another. Their exultation gave way to a woeful gloom when he told them what he had seen.

" Eschwege dead ! Our Eschwege dead ! We can't believe that ! "

The officer nodded.

" We will not believe it. And we have still cause to hope that he is only wounded ! Yes, perhaps not even that ! Perhaps his engine only stopped when he was flying away from the cloud of the explosion, and he landed safely somewhere over there."

Then all hearts took courage again. If only that was so !

. . . . .

About noon Lieutenant König rang me up from Drama.

His voice sounded so tired that I thought of Eschwege at once, for we were continually anxious on his behalf. And then he gave me the report from the Bulgarian artillery observation post.

A small spark of hope still glowed in us, but it was very, very tiny. The Bulgarian report left open the possibility that Eschwege might have come down alive, even though wounded.

But why did not the balloon burn slowly, according to the rule?

There was only one possibility; the English had filled the basket with explosives and ignited it by means of a cable at the moment when Eschwege had to pass close over the top of the balloon after his successful attack. The " observer " in the basket was only a stuffed dummy.

Later on, our theory was confirmed by the statements of prisoners and the official report of the activities of the 16th Wing. The latter account states :

" When three (!) balloons had been shot down in flames, an unserviceable envelope was sent up. The basket contained a heavy bomb, which was calculated to bring down any machine within a radius of a hundred yards when it exploded. This was connected up with the observers on the ground by means of an electric cable.

" When an enemy scout attacked the balloon on November 21st, 1917, and came close to it, the charge was ignited, so that the machine broke up. The subsequent investigation confirmed the supposition that the machine was flown by Lieutenant von Eschwege, the most successful German pilot on this front."

.   .   .   .   .

An English airman appeared over Drama in the afternoon and dropped a streamer. In the weighted bag attached to it was found a letter, written in German with the following contents :

" To the Bulgarian-German Flying Corps in Drama.

" The officers of the Royal Flying Corps regret to announce that Lieutenant von Eschwege was killed while attacking the captive balloon. His personal belongings will be dropped over the lines some time during the next few days."

A few days later an Englishman sent a second streamer fluttering down.

It contained the photographs of Eschwege's funeral. He was buried by the English with full military honours. (Photograph 36.) Six flying officers bore his coffin.

．　　．　　．　　．　　．

The Bulgarians put up a memorial to him in Drama. It bears the following inscription :

> LIEUTENANT RUDOLF VON ESCHWEGE
> Pilot.
> Born on February 25th, 1895
> at Homburg vor der Höhe
> Fell as a hero at Orljak
> On the occasion of his twentieth aerial victory
> on November 21st, 1917.
>
> ———
>
> From the 10th Aegean Division.

The stone monument was flanked by two mighty beacons. Yet first of all the Bulgarians lit another beacon—not in Drama, but over the grave itself, in the enemy's territory, for, on March 15th, 1918, they shot down in flames the fifth captive balloon of Orljak with a shell from their long-barrelled gun—Eschwege's balloon !

And what of the other German airmen ?

In the next few months there were heavy casualties among them. Lieutenant Rottka was transferred to the Serial Photography Troop. Two English machines brought him and his pilot, Sergeant Grasmehr, down over Hristos. He escaped with some bruises and a sprained backbone.

Lieutenant Lenz flew with Flying Section 20, which took over my Staffel's sector. He and Lieutenant Hermstedt, of the Army Aircraft Park, No. 11, were ordered to take a machine from Hudova to Drama. They were shot down in flames over Sarmusakli.

Lieutenant König joined Flying Section 30 at Hudova. When spotting for artillery he was wounded in the foot by machine-gun fire from the ground.

When I received my appointment on the General Staff I was wounded in the right upper thigh on Hill 1050 by an Italian mine splinter.

Then Drama's new scout-flier, Lieutenant Hoesch, redressed the balance in our favour by a truly heroic feat.

The English put up another captive balloon at Orljak a few days after the success scored by the Bulgarian artillerymen. There was a strong presumption that it might be laden with explosives.

Nevertheless, Hoesch attacked it on March 20th— and for the sixth time an envelope went up in flames. The glowing shreds which floated across to the hero's grave in the vicinity were a more beautiful adornment than any red roses, while the odour of the burning was sweeter than the sharp scent of laurel wreaths.

Map showing localities in War Flying in Macedonia

Many names appearing on this map will differ from those used in English atlases. Most places marked on it had three names,—a Greek, a Turkish and a Bulgarian, so that it was a matter of pure chance which name was used by the two opposing forces. Whenever it was possible to identify a name with a different name for the same place used in the Times Atlas, I have substituted the latter for the reader's convenience. When there was any doubt, it seemed to me better to leave the names used in Captain Heydemarck's map. Translator's Note.

o   Towns
∴   Ruins
∼   Lakes
⊥   Marshes
═   Roads
∼   Paths
▬   Railways
∞   German & Bulgarian Aerodromes
⊶   Aerodromes
♈   Captive Balloons ⎫ English
▬   Warships   ⎬
▄▄   English Front   ⎭

Scale
10   0   10   20   30   40 km